D1168596

"David Wardell and Jeff Leever have provided tools for discipleship, whether you are the discipler or the one being discipled. . . Whether you are a man or a woman, you will find encouragement to keep the fire burning."

DEE BRESTIN, Heritage Keepers speaker
and author of *The Friendships of Women*

"If you will dare to 'enter in' to this teaching, don't be surprised if you find yourself reaching levels of spiritual maturity of which you've only dreamed of before. One thing is unmistakably clear: Jesus calls all that believe in Him into rigorous, uncompromising discipleship–to *'take up his cross and follow me.'* This book will help you fulfill that call."

BILL MCCARTNEY,
president of Promise Keepers
and author of *Sold Out*

"When Dave Wardell writes about discipleship, he has my full attention. Dave has been discipling in the trenches of life for thirty years. He knows of what he speaks."

DR. STEVE FARRAR, president of
Men's Leadership Ministries
and author of *Get in the Ark*

"One of our basic human drives is to have wholesome relationships. *Daily Disciples* is a powerful resource to help guide you into building relationships of integrity, intelligence, and pure godly intimacy."

THELMA WELLS,
Women of Faith speaker and author

"Dave Wardell has tackled a much needed task–and has succeeded. There is no more important need in the church today than to help believers measure up to the stature of Jesus Christ."

DR. GENE GETZ, pastor and author of
The Measure of a Man and *The Measure of a Woman*

"While Joshua was herald to the spotlight and upfront leadership, we've always wondered about Caleb's 'in the background experiences.' Well, in this book, *Daily Disciples,* you can read the firsthand account of a modern Caleb (David Wardell) in the seeming shadow of his Joshua (Bill McCartney) and learn how, at the appointed time, he was ready to 'take the mountain,' as you can be, too."

BISHOP PHILLIP PORTER,
former chairman of the board,
Promise Keepers

"This book will help you to be a disciple and to be a discipler. Thanks, Dave and Jeff, for giving us a hand to guide us around the pitfalls of life, a cheer to keep us going when we get weary, and a roadmap to help us stay the course."

LAURIE HALL,
author of *An Affair of the Mind* and
The Cleavers Don't Live Here Anymore

Daily
DISCIPLES

Daily DISCIPLES

*Growing Every Day as a
Follower of Christ*

David B. Wardell, Ph.D.
and
Jeffrey A. Leever

PROMISE
P R E S S
An Imprint of Barbour Publishing

Published by Promise Press, an imprint of Barbour Publishing, Inc., P.O. Box 719, Uhrichsville, Ohio 44683, www.promisepress.com

Member of the
Evangelical Christian
Publishers Association

Printed in the United States of America.

DEDICATION

*In memory of Rod Marable & Joel England
—into His presence, August 8, 1998*

CONTENTS

FOREWORD

For more than seventeen years now, I've had the privilege of knowing Dave Wardell as a brother in Christ, friend, and colaborer in ministry. I am very excited he has finally written a book on discipleship.

Dave is one of the men almighty God has used at critical junctures to shape my faith and the direction of my life. When I arrived in Colorado in 1982 as football coach of the University of Colorado Buffaloes, Dave was among the first to befriend me. While others understandably took a "wait and see" approach, Dave reached out, took me under his wing, and became a spiritual mentor. An immediate rapport developed between us. In his work with the Fellowship of Christian Athletes (FCA) at the university, he was in a strategic position to introduce me to other Christians in the community and to help me find the fellowship I so desperately needed.

As some may be aware, a conversation I had with Dave led to the birth of the Promise Keepers movement. While Dave and I made a fateful three-hour car ride from Boulder to an FCA banquet in Pueblo, Colorado, in the spring of 1990, we had a life-changing discussion about our true passions for ministry. The gist of this was the answer to this question: "What would you most like to see God do in your lifetime?" My response was to see stadiums filled with men worshiping and glorifying God. Without hesitation, Dave said his heart's desire was to see others discipled for Christ. I knew Dave well enough to know he was being absolutely honest. This was a transparent, face-to-face conversation. The Lord's calling for Dave's life ministry was abundantly clear.

While Promise Keepers has become famous for bringing large Christian gatherings together, it has always been plain to us that real spiritual growth and change do not generally take place apart from vital *relationships.* In fact, for any participant to attend a PK event and come away believing that he can achieve maturity in Christ—or to be a promise keeper—without being involved with others in a discipleship process of some kind is wishful thinking, at best.

For the great majority of Christians, whether women or men, the fact is that a one-time experience—however spiritually significant—does not have the staying power to produce lasting change in their lives. Some might point to Moses at the burning bush or to the Apostle Paul's "Damascus Road" experience as exceptions, but that's the point—they were exceptions to the rule. These were individuals whose lives God impacted in an extraordinary way. On the other hand, most of us need the encouragement and accountability others can provide just to resist and conquer sin in our lives, much less to be *all* God calls us to be! And I believe God has always intended that the Body of Christ here on earth depend on one another.

Jesus demonstrated the importance of this dynamic by surrounding Himself with the first "local church" group, the twelve disciples. As this community of commoners learned of Christ together, they were transformed into people who individually and collectively "turned the world upside down!" After spending three years being taught by Jesus, and then filled with the power of the Holy Spirit, the disciples were ready to *"go and make disciples of all nations."* And they did, spreading the gospel throughout the known world of their day. That's the power of the local church, of men and women gathering together around the person of Christ, learning of God's Word, and helping each other apply it to their lives. That's the power of discipleship! It's the biblical means to bring about positive change in the everyday lives of believers—or in the lives of everyday believers.

I wholeheartedly agree with Dave Wardell that in order to

see Christians achieve maturity in Christ, someone—a mature Christian, a mentor, a discipler—must come alongside them. In other words, spiritual change and growth are designed to take place in the context of dynamic relationship with other believers. When the thrill of the conference is over, the last worship song is sung, the stage comes down, and the lights are turned off, this is how the Church and our society will be transformed.

Daily Disciples is the book "Dr. Dave" was born to write. It's his opus, his lifework, his grand contribution to a movement of God's Spirit in our land today. As you read through and study this inspired publication, know that it comes from a man who lives what he says. Dave loves Jesus with all his heart and loves other human beings as well—with a yearning to help them reach their full potential in Christ. Dave is a guy who cares deeply about others and about relationships. What he has written here comes out of a lifetime of experience both as a disciple and a discipler of others.

As you read this book and digest the wisdom, encouragement, and teaching Dave has to offer, I know you will be blessed. More importantly, as you prayerfully consider how the Lord might want you to be involved in discipleship as a "discipler/mentor," a "disciplee," or simply as a member of a fellowship group (or all three), you will grow spiritually. In fact, if you will dare to "enter in" to this teaching, don't be surprised if you find yourself reaching levels of spiritual maturity of which you've only dreamed before. One thing is unmistakably clear: Jesus calls all that believe in Him into rigorous, uncompromising discipleship—to *"take up his cross and follow me."* This book will help you fulfill that call.

BILL McCARTNEY
president of Promise Keepers
and author of *Sold Out*

INTRODUCTION

I've seen what Promise Keepers can do in the heart of a man, lighting a spark that causes him to love his God, his family, and his brothers in Christ with a renewed passion. But when the conference is over, when the days turn into months, what keeps the flame from growing low and eventually disappearing? This same question applies to women I've seen come back from Women of Faith, Time Out for Women, Heritage Keepers, or other women's events.

If we are alone, we are like a single log, and the flame will soon die. But if we find a sister or brother, perhaps one whose flame has burned longer and brighter—and if we find yet another sister or brother, someone whose flame has burned shorter and dimmer—then we will kindle each other, the sparks will leap from one to another, and the fire in our hearts will burn brightly, spreading warmth to our homes, our churches, and our world. Recording artist Kathy Troccoli commented to me, "We say we want friends who will sharpen us, but we don't really. We don't want friends who will tell us the truth." One of the aspects I so appreciate about *Daily Disciples* is that you will be encouraged to seek out friends of your own gender and to speak the truth in love to one another. And it is God's truth that has the power to truly set us free.

David Wardell and Jeff Leever have provided tools for discipleship, whether you are the discipler or the one being discipled. Prayerfully consider whom the Lord would have you meet with –perhaps on a weekly basis to discuss the chapter or to do the lesson in the *Daily Disciples Study Guide*. Whether you are a man or a woman, you will find encouragement to keep the fire burning.

If you are hesitant—as is sometimes especially true of men— to meet with another and make yourself vulnerable, I would encourage you to consider the model of Jesus. He not only discipled twelve men (and look how the ripples spread!), He found encouragement Himself through a smaller circle of three (Peter, James, and John). He made himself vulnerable, He wept, He laughed, He expressed His love. He allowed His life to flow into them, and from them, into the world. He has asked you to follow in His steps, and *Daily Disciples* will show you how.

DEE BRESTIN
author of *The Friendships of Women*
and *Falling in Love with Jesus* (with KATHY TROCCOLI)

ACKNOWLEDGMENTS

DAVE: I would like to thank Jay and Marti Oertli (Navigators) for their discipleship of my wife and me. I want to acknowledge Dan Stavely (Fellowship of Christian Athletes), Chuck Lane (Campus Crusade for Christ), and Dan Schaffer (Building Brothers) for their discipleship. The men in my accountability small group—Cliff Martin, Jim Messmer, and Berk Sterling—are deserving of much thanks. Thanks as well to Ed Nava, another accountability partner of mine. Also I thank Pastor Tom Alexander of Cherry Hills Community Church and Pastor Jim Amend of Southside United Protestant Church for their discipleship and encouragement. In addition, Eric Wardell has helped me grow in accountability and discipleship, and as a parent. And finally, above all, I want to acknowledge my best friend and "life partner," Carolyn Wardell, for the thirty-seven years of discipleship I have shared with her.

JEFF: Much thanks should go first to my wife Erin (what a woman!), who in the book's earliest stages read the chapters before anyone else, as they were written, and helped catch more things in need of change than I might ever care to admit. With the first few chapters in particular, I am thankful for the editing eye of my coworker and former fellow writer, Tim Zastrocky. I would also like to extend gratitude to Alvin Simpkins and Eric Wardell for taking part in the initial storyboard session that helped serve as a guide for the content of this book. In addition, I appreciate the willingness to help demonstrated by Sharalee Rediger and Joy Meyer, Dave's assistants during the span of the manuscript's initial creation; also Terry Bey, Mac's writer. Finally, kudos to the Rev. James Amend for his leadership, support, and encouragement.

PROLOGUE

Dreaming. . .

A man. A fearful man. A tormented conscience. A series of denials. . .*from his own lips.* . .for that which yet he *knows* is the most important thing in his life.

How could this happen?

Tears.

Then, more tears.

Anguish.

He can't stand it.

A man confounded by his conflicted moments of passion and zeal, hesitancy and doubt.

What will he do. . . ?

Peter, shoulder to shoulder with other early disciples, will go on to become one of the foremost communicators of the message of Christ.

In the court is a woman who lives in pain. She has money and worldly influence. But that is never enough. Never enough to heal her hurt, fill her void.

Not only has she suffered from physical pain in her life, but emotionally she's been devastated as well. She was sickened to see that a holy man was just beheaded for speaking the truth to some in her social circle. Worse, some very close to her were involved in this savage act.

Her life is uncertain, filled with pain. . . .

What will happen to her? Where can she turn?

Joanna turns to Christ, as a follower and disciple of Him, and eventually becomes one of the women present at the resurrection.

Failure. Nearly everyone has lost trust in him. He is only a young man, once so close to ostensible greatness, but while others in his fold pressed on, he quit.

Quit. For no good reason.

"No regrets," the young man tried to tell himself at first.

His denial didn't work.

Will anyone ever have faith in him again?

Is failure final?

Will he ever accomplish anything of value in this world? After all, he's now well known as a person not worth believing in. . . .

Mark gets another chance, because Barnabas, a brother in Christ, never gives up on him. Mark goes on to recommit himself to Christ and live as a true disciple. His life is no longer a failure. Today he is known as one of the four Gospel writers.

She is a woman in a culture where widespread respect for her gender simply doesn't exist. And yet she is known throughout her community for her kindness and generosity toward others.

20

Despite all the stumbling blocks in her way as a female, she's committed herself to overcoming prejudice. . .to having a soft heart regardless of circumstance. . .to loving others. She's committed herself to serving the One and only.

Still, something grave is about to descend upon her. Illness. . . Death?

A life of good intentions. . .will it be for naught. . . ?

Tabitha, in her darkest hour, is touched and healed by a disciple. As a disciple of Christ herself, she goes on to become an even greater witness to others than she had been before she fell ill.

Another young man agonizes with anxiety about his life circumstance. He has strong beliefs deep inside. . .he wants to *do something* with them. He doesn't know where to start. He's confounded.

The culture he walks in daily is all wrong. Oppressive. Dangerous. . .

Two older men, men he looked up to, were beaten and left for dead. Worse, this took place in his own backyard—a community environment he lives in but feels powerless against. Many hate the very things the young man holds dear.

What will he do? How can he overcome?

His natural timidity and fear leave him frustrated and listless. . . .

Through Christ and the encouragement of other disciples, Timothy overcame his fear. By being alongside other disciples, he grew up in his faith and made a difference in the early days of the Church. He grew so much, in fact, that he went on to teach and correct other disciples.

Like these men and women, do you struggle to overcome the problems in your life? Does the weakness of your own nature trip you up again and again? Do you find yourself wondering if there is an answer for your life's problems?

Is there hope?

How can a miracle be worked?

A change?

Someone once lived who made a difference. The ultimate difference.

Some called him Teacher. They bore witness to the healing power of His hands. All it took was a mere touch; He could cure even the worst ailment. Yet more incredible, He could do even the impossible: He had the power to overcome death.

Still, some hated Him. Mocked Him. Feared Him.

He was either the best thing ever available to the human race—or the most deluded individual ever to walk.

Despised.

Beloved.

During His time on earth, many desperately needed miracles in their lives. Words cannot begin to capture their level of desperation. He delivered.

Crowds were drawn to Him. The religious plotted against Him. Through it all, He remained steadfast. Solid in purpose. A model for everyone. He never encountered a single soul in need of a miracle beyond what He could do for them. He lived for everyone. For all time. An example. Today He still brings hope to all people, all of us who at one point or another, for one reason or another, need a miracle in our lives. He is Someone Who will deliver us from the darkness.

A Savior. A teacher. Someone we can learn from. *The* Teacher.

He left behind a legacy. He left behind a model for *Life*. *The Answer* to our lives' confusion lies in Him.

And as His body on earth–His Church–we carry this answer to each other. If we follow in His footsteps, we are His disciples. His Spirit lives in our lives, giving us the strength to *disciple* others–to reach out to others with encouragement and hope.

APPLICATIONS TO DAILY LIFE

1. When did someone reach out to you with encouragement and hope? What was your relationship with that individual? What were the circumstances?

2. To whom do you want to reach out with encouragement and hope? What is your relationship with that individual? What are the circumstances?

dai•ly adj. 1. Every day.

dis•ci•ple n. 1. A person who believes in and helps disseminate the teachings of a master. 2. Often Disciple. One of Christ's followers.

from *Webster's II New Riverside Dictionary*

CHAPTER 1

The Essence of Being a Daily Disciple

*"So come on,
let's leave the preschool fingerpainting exercises on Christ
and get on with the grand work of art.
Grow up in Christ.
The basic foundational truths are in place. . . .
But there's so much more.
Let's get on with it!"*
HEBREWS 6:1–3 THE MESSAGE

I t's the life you've always wanted for yourself, but just didn't
know how to access it.

It's the life you've thought you needed, but couldn't put your
finger on it.

Something sweeter. . .

Something vibrant. . .

What does it look like?

Imagine for a moment a picture quite unlike any you have
ever seen, a place where every man and woman has one thing
in common: They are all mature Christians. They live out the
Christ in the word *Christian* every day—in every tiny, practical
aspect of their lives. Each of them epitomizes the word *saint*.
They are bona fide followers and imitators of a carpenter called
Jesus of Nazareth.

Jesus. . .

A man who walked and talked and lived many years ago.

We have all heard of Him; perhaps we think we know Him.

He is the one human being who lived without ever once committing a sin. A Man, the Son of the living God, Who did something—something critical for all of humanity—before He went to be with the Father. He spent three years investing Himself in close relationships with twelve people—sharing Himself—so that you and I, today, would know about the love of God. So that you and I, today, could *know* Jesus.

What happened back then that was so critical?

The answer is this: God began to change lives. Through His Son's tangible presence, through His Son's relationship with those around Him, God began to complete the plan He had in mind since the earliest days of earth. He gave us a face to show us the way—a human face, the face of Jesus.

At Antioch, the followers of Christ were first called Christians (Acts 11:26). Some two thousand years later, God is still creating a movement of His people. The foundation of this movement is still Jesus.

Jesus Christ set us the example. And when we become His followers, we live the disciple's life.

It's the life you've always wanted for yourself but haven't known how to pursue.

Many Christians don't understand what it means to be a true disciple of Jesus, much less how to undertake their own spiritual growth. Some just don't think they need the disciple's life. They may have heard the term *discipleship* and thought, *Ick, sounds like work.* Others may have heard it and thought, *Huh? That sounds like something you study at seminary.* Still others want to pursue this life, but they don't know how.

Why is this thing I call the disciple's life so important? The answer to that question is critical for every Christian to know and understand. In practical terms, how do we pursue the disciple's life–this life we've always wanted?

SOMETHING BETTER FOR YOUR LIFE

Many Christians have at least heard of something called the Great Commission, found in Matthew 28:19–20: " 'Therefore go and make disciples of all nations. . .teaching them to obey everything I have commanded you. And surely I am with you always, to the very end of the age.' " But how do we do this if we don't have a clue where to begin? How can we make others disciples?

First, we have to *be disciples* ourselves. We have to live the life.

All too often people seem to assume that when Jesus says, "Go and make disciples of all nations," all He's really asking them to do is occasionally contribute financially to overseas missions projects or something similar. This definition of long-distance discipleship fails to include intimate one-on-one relationships.

How tragic! Those of us who live in the United States need only look at the rampant immorality of our culture to see the fruit of this. Worse yet, we have a Church that is full of individuals who get up in the morning every Sunday, come to a service, sit in the pew, sing the songs, listen to the sermon, go home, and *nothing changes.* Why? They have never been actively committed to the lifelong process of being a disciple.

Well, what does this thing–the life of a disciple–look like? First of all, a disciple's life is a personal growth process toward maturity in Christ (through relationships, the Word, and prayer). Along the way, as we grow, we can also have godly influence in others' lives.

Why bother? Because the truth is, many of us who have accepted Christ still feel something of a void—a longing in our soul. We sense that we are missing something. There's a deeper heart issue we need to face. That's why we go to conferences, hop from church to church, become involved in various social activities, go to a counselor, buy a book, and so on. In the deepest depths of our soul we are longing to know God more intimately, but we don't know how.

The Bible tells us to fix our eyes on "what is unseen," rather than what is seen (2 Corinthians 4:18). But how many of us actually do that? If non-Christian observers followed us through our day, what would they conclude? Do we live as though we truly have inner peace, or do we live as though we still feel something is missing?

My suspicion is that we may still feel a void, because even though we've accepted Christ's payment for our sin, we are still trying to fill ourselves up to a certain level with worldly things. We've perhaps done this in a way that is completely unintentional, but nevertheless we've still tried to fill the void on our own. We're not depending totally on Jesus; our focus is still on the things that are "seen" rather than "unseen." Not surprisingly, how does this make us feel in the end? Hollow.

In the Christian journey through life, I believe we're either moving closer to God every day, or we're moving away from Him. The choice is ours. We all have a responsibility to grow in Christ. We can't—*you can't*—afford to ignore the longing of our souls. . .that sense that we need to be closer to Him.

Oswald Chambers, in his classic work *My Utmost for His*

Highest, says this:
> *One life wholly devoted to God is of more value to God than*
> *one hundred lives simply awakened by His Spirit.*[1]

A disciple—someone *living* the life of a disciple—is first and foremost a follower of Christ. Not just a follower of some of His teachings, but also a follower of the Man Himself. A disciple is wholly devoted to Him.

CHRIST'S IMPACT

Jesus Christ came and spent time with His apostles for three years and impacted them in such a way that the world would never be the same. He is our spiritual leader and model; we need to pattern our behavior and walk after His example. The early disciples followed Him so closely that they were willing to die for Him—and many of them did.

Human history has been forever changed by Christ's influence. Even people today who deny His name do not hesitate to put the year "2001" as part of the date. History itself has been divided into before Christ (B.C.) and *anno Domini* (A.D.)—in the year of our Lord—just one small detail that validates Jesus' influence on world history.

The most important world changes, however, were wrought by Christ in hearts and lives. His effectiveness in His relationships is undeniable, even by atheistic standards. He set an example of how to truly love human beings. Not just any example, but the one best example for people for all time. He epitomized "God is love."

As disciples of Christ, then, we, too, must seek to live lives controlled by love. Again, a disciple follows all aspects of Christ—His teachings, His examples—everything that He left us.

WATERING SPIRITUAL SEEDS

While He was on earth, Jesus Christ was an example to His disciples every day. They had a chance to interact and learn from His life experiences. The disciples spent *three years* with Jesus. Yet after the crucifixion, it looked like the disciples were going to quit and disband. Some went into hiding in fear of the Romans, but Jesus' example had sown the spiritual seed. Even though it looked like the movement was finished, God's seed would germinate after Pentecost.

One grandmother tells the story of some "seeds" that did not germinate for many years:

I first began to pray for my granddaughter when she was a day old. I held her in my arms and I asked God that He would keep her always close to Himself. Although her parents had no time for God, they allowed me to take her to church with me every Sunday. From the time she was a tiny thing until she was a teenager, she and I would go to church. Afterward, we would sing and pray together as we got the Sunday meal.

But then my granddaughter moved away to go to college. I didn't see her much anymore, but I knew she wasn't living the way God wanted her to. I guess she still called herself a Christian, but she certainly wasn't growing in the Lord. I just kept praying for her, though, trusting that God would send people into her life that would water the seeds of faith in her heart.

I'm sad to say that my granddaughter went through long years of heartache and sin. But just this year, on her fortieth birthday, she called me up. "I've got good news," she said. She didn't say anything more for a few seconds, and I thought she was crying, but it sounded like tears of joy. And then she said, "I've been going to church again, Grandma. People have been helping me grow in the Lord. I never dreamed following Jesus could be so sweet."

Proverbs 22:6 tells us, "Train a child in the way he should go, and when he is old he will not turn from it." While many of us are no longer children in the physical sense, many of us are still immature spiritually. Like the granddaughter in this story, we, too, have been "planted," yet we fail to grow. Spiritual training still needs to occur for every human being. Steve Farrar states, "In the Christian life, it's not how you start that matters. It's how you finish."[2] How do we finish a marathon when we haven't made a serious investment in training? How do we *finish* with our faith *strong* if we never go into spiritual training? (See 1 Corinthians 3:2, Hebrews 5:12, 1 Peter 2:2.)

But how do we go into spiritual training? In practical terms, what does daily discipleship look like? These are some of the questions that will be addressed through the course of this book. Basically, though, I believe the disciple's life consists of three key components, all equally important: relationships, the Word, and prayer.

RELATIONSHIPS

I 'm not talking here about just a casual or recreational relationship but a committed relationship. The kind of relationship the Bible is talking about in Proverbs 17:17: "A friend is
always loyal. . .is born to help in time of need" (NLT). And again
in Proverbs: "As iron sharpens iron, a friend sharpens a friend"
(27:17 NLT). While there may be nothing wrong with just "getting to know" others, or going out "just to have fun" and building relationships that way, if we look at the Word, we see that
maturity begins with *a sound commitment.*

In the context of the disciple's life, one thing needs to be
pointed out. Committed relationships don't just happen instantly; we can't simply pop into each other's lives and begin to
disciple each other. This sort of relationship takes time and trust
to develop. The initial focus is on the relationship; down the
road as the relationship develops is where we can begin to help
one another grow as disciples.

I know an old coach here in Colorado, Dan Stavely, who
personifies the type of committed relationship development
that is so vital to the disciple's life. He's eighty-seven years old
with a body that's feeling its age, but his mind is still sharp and
focused on God's Word. Over the past thirty years, he has
brought about more change in men and women than most
major ministries. He'll invest in relationships with college students for eight hours a day. One person will come see him at 8
A.M., another at nine, another student comes in at ten, and so
on. He meets with students from three different Colorado uni-
versities one-on-one, for one hour, once a week.

What would motivate him to do that? Wouldn't it seem

more logical for him to get everybody together to give them the message all at once? After all, ministries like Women of Faith and Promise Keepers have attempted to give the message in venues of up to seventy thousand participants. Much good for the body of Christ has certainly come out of this fellowship—but meetings like these *alone* do not necessarily bring with them intimacy, vital relationships, or the disciple's life. Too many Christians who come back home from these conferences have been emotionally inspired but spiritually nothing changes in their lives.

Long-term change will happen in our lives only when I begin to meet with you and we become mutually committed to one another and to the disciple's life. This takes time! One-on-one or small group relationships, over time, can change lives and provide an atmosphere for spiritual growth.

THE WORD

T he second component in the disciple's life is God's Word: "For the word of God is living and active. Sharper than any double-edged sword, it penetrates even to dividing soul and spirit, joints and marrow; it judges the thoughts and attitudes of the heart" (Hebrews 4:12). Also, in 2 Timothy 3:16 we read, "All Scripture is God-breathed and is useful for teaching, rebuking, correcting and training in righteousness."

Many people know the first part of what Jesus said in the Great Commission, about how we should go and make disciples. What comes after this is the key: *". . .teaching them to obey everything I have commanded you."* We can't simply drop the Good News of Christ on people like a bomb and then go on our merry way. We need to stick around and truly love people—and the end purpose must be encouraging each other to be obedient to Jesus' teachings. This means that any kind of small group formed, if it is to be truly biblical, cannot miss the mark on this one. The focus of our relationships in Christ cannot be merely good times and emotional bonding. We must be reading and meditating on the Bible, helping each other apply its lessons to practical living situations.

PRAYER

The third component for the disciple's life is prayer. God says to us His children, "Cry out to Me!" Of course He already knows everything our hearts desire and need, but we need to bring our concerns to Him in prayer. In Philippians 4:19, He promises He "will meet all your needs according to his glorious riches in Christ Jesus." The disciple's life unfolds in a meaningful and clear way—one that has a direction—when we access God's heart and His will through prayer.

When we go to God in prayer, we don't simply come with a list of requests. It is also up to us to ask our heavenly Father to "direct our steps." This is a decision we choose to make or not to make. He is always available to us—we can access His power and love in our lives' every detail *large or small*—but it's up to us to seek Him. He is the Author of all things. All blessings. Prayer opens up the floodgates in our lives like nothing else can.

Remember the three components: relationships, the Word, and prayer. As we spend time with Christ, through prayer and the Word, with other Christians, we literally begin the journey of life that is the *disciple's life.*

APPLICATIONS TO DAILY LIFE

1. Are you feeling a void–a longing in your soul and in your life?

2. In assessing where you are in your spiritual journey, consider the three components of being a daily disciple:

    Relationships: Do you have committed relationships in your life? With whom? Do you think of these relationships as part of your life as a daily disciple?

    Word: Are you spending time reading and meditating on the Bible?

    Prayer: Do you pray daily? Have you asked God to give you an attitude of prayer?

CHAPTER 2

The Cost of Daily Discipleship

*"I will not sacrifice to the LORD my God
burnt offerings that cost me nothing."*
2 SAMUEL 24:24

B eing Christ's follower on a daily, moment-by-moment
basis is the most rewarding way to live. In fact, it's the
lifestyle for which we were each created. But it's not always
easy. It will cost us something.

Most of us have not counted the cost of being committed to
Christ in a way that affects our lives very deeply in our families, our friendships, our work, or even our church. Jesus
addressed this issue in Luke 14:28–33:

> *"Suppose one of you wants to build a tower. Will he not first
> sit down and estimate the cost to see if he has enough money
> to complete it? For if he lays the foundation and is not able
> to finish it, everyone who sees it will ridicule him, saying,
> 'This fellow began to build and was not able to finish.'*
>
> *"Or suppose a king is about to go to war against another
> king. Will he not first sit down and consider whether he is
> able with ten thousand men to oppose the one coming against
> him with twenty thousand? If he is not able, he will send a
> delegation while the other is still a long way off and will ask
> for terms of peace. In the same way, any of you who does not
> give up everything he has cannot be my disciple."*

41

A perfect example of the classic "failure to count the cost" situation was shared with me recently. A gentleman from California wrote to Promise Keepers and told of his efforts to become involved in a small group through his church. Much to his dismay, this "Bible study" group made drinking beer a regular part of their meetings. The man approached the group's leader and explained that he was a recovering alcoholic and asked if they would cease making the consumption of alcoholic beverages a part of their fellowship time. The leader basically told the man to "get over it"–the booze would continue to be a part of their meetings! Clearly, the members of this group failed to "count the cost" of being Christ's disciples.

I do not know what happened in the end to the recovering alcoholic. He may have given up altogether on building relationships. Or maybe he sought out another avenue for Christian fellowship. Each response would indicate something about him. Perhaps he had maturity that exceeded that of those in the group he initially attempted to join. Perhaps not.

The pursuit of the disciple's life almost always strikes a blow to our self-centered habits. Are we willing to give up our own agenda and let God have His way with us? How about you? Have you ever let the behavior of others deter you from pursuing the disciple's life? Have you counted the cost of being Christ's disciple?

If a fellowship spectrum exists–with one end being *biblical* fellowship, the other *secular* fellowship–the booze incident illustrates how far some Christians are from where they should be. Getting together just for the sake of beer and chatter may have value to some people from an entertainment or recreational standpoint, but where is Jesus? Bonding is not all there is to the disciple's life.

We also fail to count the cost in other, more subtle ways.

In the Gospels, we read of Martha, a woman who was so focused on the things "she should be doing" with her time that she failed to allow Christ to minister to her and work in her life. Jesus spoke to her and tried to help her understand that the life He wanted for her wasn't one consumed by the "many things" of life. He wanted her to see that all those busy responsibilities weren't as important as simply being in His presence.

Adrian Boyd is a churchgoing woman, much like many women today, who has found herself needing to take time to *intentionally* not be like Martha. She says, "There are many women whom I know, some I'm in Bible study with, who never seem to count the cost of being a disciple of Christ. I've had to make sure that my 'real work'—or any other activity that might distract me from growing closer to Christ—is kept in the proper perspective. I mean, who am I really trying to impress by having a tidy house, or a 'together' life? God or people? If I get myself too busy to study my Bible, notice my husband, or simply call a friend, then I'm missing the point."

Of course, Adrian doesn't mean that we should simply neglect work that needs to be done. But we should never allow ourselves to be fooled into thinking some of the constant tasks we pursue are going to produce something of long-term importance. The work that expresses Christ's love to others, the work that we offer up to Him in love as His disciple, that is the only work that has eternal importance in the spiritual realm.

WHAT SHOULD I DO?

B ut when we talk about counting the cost in relation to our life as daily disciples, we don't mean that Christ's followers need to be ruled by legalism; we want God's Holy Spirit to control our lives, not a whole list of "shoulds" and "shouldn'ts."

In the body of Christ, you can always find someone willing to tell you a version of this statement: You *should* do more (read more, evangelize more, go to church more, and so on). Is the disciple's life more of the same song? Or. . .just possibly. . . could it be. . .*different?*

Yes!

God has given us a wonderful opportunity to have a closer relationship with Him, an opportunity to be more like Jesus Christ. This isn't one more thing we *should* do in order to somehow prove our worth, one more thing to consume our already busy lives. Instead, this is something that enriches our lives. We benefit!

Does that mean we might have to "do something" different than what we would normally? Most likely. (That's where the cost comes in.) Yet I believe—and I think it will become clear through this book—that the disciple's life is for our own good. We're missing out on soothing medicine for our soul when we don't pursue it.

As we read in Luke, most of us have not counted the cost of this medicine. I'm not saying, however, that walking in relationship with Christ is something we can earn, something we can buy with our good behavior. No, grace is free. But to get from immaturity to maturity in the Christian life, I believe Christ must increase in our lives and we must decrease (John

3:30). We must actively pursue God's heart and will.

Too Busy Not to Be Discipled

Some people may say to me, "But, Dave, I hear what you are saying, I want to grow in Christ, but I just don't think I have the *time* to invest in this." This is one excuse that's so common in our American culture; it's the most common excuse I hear when I challenge others. But truly, the lack of time is not the real issue. *The real issue is your use of time.* As disciples, we use our time more effectively. If we are following in Christ's footsteps, what we do really counts for something.

The disciple's life also happens to be exciting! I've been created—you have been created and put on this earth—to do something, for the cause of God's kingdom. As Christians, we have been given a purpose. . .we already have a direction. . .a mandate to pursue. This should be fuel for our soul to motivate us to press on (Philippians 3:14). Together, we encourage and inspire each other to keep growing personally, building the Kingdom together.

In Ephesians 4:12 we find affirmation for the purpose of living a disciple's life: "to equip the saints for the work of ministry, for building up the body of Christ" (NRSV). As Jack Hayford has observed, "There is nothing more fundamental to the teaching of Jesus Christ than that you can never make it alone."[1] We need each other on this journey.

But like any journey, you have to first set out on your trip. If you never begin, you'll never reach your destination.

THE NARROW ROAD FOUND ONLY BY A FEW

How do we begin this journey? By accepting Christ into our lives and hearts.

There are men and women who make a lot of money, and from a worldly, physical standpoint they look very successful. Many of them, in reality, have had two or three divorces, or perhaps their kids are on drugs. They might be making millions, but they have made no spiritual impact on the lives of others. They don't know the abundant life. People like this would give anything to have real peace, "the peace. . .which transcends all understanding" (Philippians 4:7). The problem is they usually go about finding peace incorrectly. Only peace and joy in the Lord Jesus Christ bring the abundant life (John 10:10). There is no other way (John 14:6).

Once you receive Christ, you receive the Spirit of God in you. As soon as you receive Him, you are a new creation (2 Corinthians 5:17), a different person. Your emotions and feelings do not determine whether or not you are a different person. You are! That's a promise of God. God didn't send His only Son to die for your sins—nor did the Son of God rise from the dead—so you could say, "I'm not a new creation, I don't really have a new life because I do not *feel* like it." He gave you an opportunity for a new life. The life of a disciple. The disciple's life!

At what point are you today? Are you experiencing the abundant life? You *can* experience this life. We can get there *together.*

"Enter through the narrow gate. For wide is the gate and broad is the road that leads to destruction, and many enter

*through it. But small is the gate and narrow the road that
leads to life, and only a few find it.*"

JESUS CHRIST in
the Gospel of Matthew (7:13–14)

APPLICATIONS TO DAILY LIFE

B efore you conclude this chapter, I would like to ask you
to think about six questions. These questions will help
you assess where you are in your spiritual journey.

1. What matters most in your life?

2. Have you ever made a difference in anybody's life?

3. Do you have a close friend (one who loves you, but is
   not impressed by you)?

4. What was your earthly father like and how has that
   affected your relationship with your heavenly
   Father?

5. Have you ever given a blessing to a son/daughter or
   been the recipient of their blessing?

6. What do you want your epitaph on your gravestone to
   say (especially if it were written by your family and
   close friends)?

Be brutally honest when thinking about your answers. Allow the Holy Spirit to bring to your mind anything you need to act upon to come into alignment with God's will in your life. How do your answers to these questions relate to what we have discussed so far about the disciple's life? Is the seed God planted in your life growing?

CHAPTER 3

Relationships

See to it. . .that none of you has a sinful,
unbelieving heart that turns away from the living God.
But encourage one another daily, as long as it is called Today,
so that none of you may be hardened by sin's deceitfulness.
We have come to share in Christ if we hold firmly
till the end the confidence we had at first.
HEBREWS 3:12–14

❖ ❖ ❖

"We are born helpless. . . .
We need others physically, emotionally, intellectually;
we need them if we are to know anything, even ourselves." [1]
C. S. LEWIS

If you were to share with a trusted friend that you struggle with watching television programming you know you shouldn't, your friend could react in a number of ways. The reaction you receive will most likely reveal the depth of your friend's commitment to you—and your friend's reaction may or may not be an example of true discipleship. As we mentioned in the opening chapter, committed relationships are at the core of living as a daily disciple. Our commitment to each other radically affects the way we interact with one another.

For instance, in the situation we just described, your friend could say to you, "Well, just turn off the TV and pray about it." In this case, your friend probably can't really relate to your problem, but he thinks telling you this will help. He might be truly concerned, however, even though he doesn't really understand. Or he may simply practice doling out "spiritual-sounding" advice in an effort to make himself seem well versed and disciplined.

On the other hand, imagine the difference if that friend makes a committed effort to help you. Think how you'll feel if your friend says to you, "Let's talk about your problem some more. Why do you think you're having this struggle? Let's pray about this together." The two of you spend some time talking over the struggle you're experiencing–and then you spend some more time beside each other in prayer. Your friend is committed to helping you. . .as long as it takes. . .until you get through this problem.

Now this is a committed relationship. The following story gives us another example of this kind of daily disciple relationship.

TWO FRIENDS

M any years ago two friends shared something difficult in common–they had each lost a spouse. One of them, though, was particularly upset with God, as she had lost not only a husband but both of her sons as well.

Shortly thereafter she told all those closest to her something like this: "Go away."

But it didn't work. Her friend wouldn't let her drift away from their relationship.

Here's what the friend said in response: " 'Where you go I will go, and where you stay I will stay. Your people will be my people and your God my God. Where you die I will die, and there I will be buried. May the LORD deal with me, be it ever so severely, if anything but death separates you and me.' "

This account of amazing commitment is from the story of

Naomi and Ruth. The quote (Ruth 1:16–17) is sometimes shared at modern-day weddings. Originally, though, these words described simply this: a committed relationship–the sort of relationship where disciples can help each other grow closer to their Lord.

Christ's twelve disciples were privileged to have Jesus physically with them all day, all night, for three years. This obviously isn't an advantage you and I have–but we do have each other. Committed relationships help us win the struggles we all encounter in our Christian life. And as Dr. Gary Rosberg states in his excellent book *Guard Your Heart*, "What is a victorious life but a series of little victorious skirmishes?"[2]

In forming relationships, many men I speak with don't know where to start. Many women I speak with may have relationships, but feel these friendships focus less on spiritual matters than on other things. Both of these situations are common. The real problem comes when we allow the statement "I don't know what to do" to mentally move to a "therefore, I cannot be expected to follow Christ's example and pursue committed relationships with others."

ONE PERSON'S TESTIMONY

Walking together as daily disciples is a life-long journey, an ongoing process. If we are willing to be committed to this process, the value of our relationships can be immeasurable. Consider the following story from the book *Brothers!* by Geoff Gorsuch and Dan Schafer. This story is titled "The Father I Never Had."

I have been involved in a men's small accountability group with four other men for approximately seventeen months. This group of men has become a source of wise counsel for me, and in many ways they have become the father I never had.

I became involved with them after a Promise Keepers Conference in Boulder, Colorado. A man named Steve called me personally and asked if I would join him and a couple of other men to meet together once a week on Wednesday mornings.

My first question: "What are you going to talk about?" Steve said they'd be talking about their marriages and specifically how to be more intimate with their wives. I asked, "What do you mean, more intimate?" He explained that we would focus on Ephesians 5:25 and then allow God to direct our steps. I already knew I wanted to change my selfish attitude and be a better husband. This looked like the opportunity I'd been waiting for to do something about it.

Well, as time passed and the commitments to each other deepened, I experienced some profound personal and spiritual changes in my life. As we began to pray, study the Word, and discuss our marriages, something unique began to take place. I began to open up to these men. I discussed my pain and the lack of confidence I was feeling as a Christian man—the husband, father, and supposed spiritual leader of my home.

These men, through their counsel, "held my feet to the fire." At first, I didn't like being told what I was really like, but now I value their counsel and have given them permission to ask me some tough questions. Because of my trust in these men, my relationship with my wife is much better. I have also been able to give my father and my sons the blessing of a much deeper relationship.

I guess I can say that on my own I never would have

*joined an accountability group. However, after being in one
for over a year, I will never be without one. Proverbs 27:17 is
the verse I've chosen which best summarizes my experience
with these men. It says, "As iron sharpens iron, so one man
sharpens another." There were moments when the "sharpen-
ing" was very painful, but I can honestly say that the pain
has been worth it.*

*As you can tell, I am now a zealot for guiding men into
small groups because without relationship and accountability,
we will never, as Christian men, reach our spiritual potential.*[3]

This man's story is not unique. More and more individuals
are discovering the value of committed relationships. One
other thing—the name of the man in this story: Dave Wardell!

As I look back, I can see a gradual progression led to my
own personal spiritual commitment to change—and each step of
this progression was inspired by a relationship with another
Christian. First, a fellow Christian challenged me to get in a
group and develop committed relationships, then I experienced personal growth within that group. . .and finally a confrontation with my wife *changed* my life.

TIME FOR SOME ACCOUNTABILITY

I ronically, one of my biggest opportunities for personal growth
came as a result of *my encouraging others* to be involved in
committed relationships.

I was just beginning to go out and speak (representing
Promise Keepers) throughout the state of Colorado. As I put

together speaking material, I read a book that included a long listing of different ways men could show love to their wives. I had written up a synopsis of that material and copied down a list of one hundred items. Then I decided, "What better way to find out if this is 'on target' than to bounce it off my wife?"

One Saturday I wasn't out speaking and was spending the day at home for a change, so I said, "Carolyn, I want to run something by you." I asked her to rate me on a scale of one to ten as I read from the list of one hundred ways to show love. I told her I wanted to know "How am I doing?" As I started down the list—I had given myself tens obviously—I was in for a rude awakening.

I didn't get past the first few questions. Already, she was ranking me at about a two or a three. I stared back at her in disbelief, but after twenty-nine years of marriage, I knew when she wasn't kidding—and this time she was dead serious. Sitting over breakfast that day, I can remember being totally stunned.

But I couldn't deny the scores my wife had given me. She had *the look* in her eyes, as the character Tim Taylor from *Home Improvement* would say. It's a look that you know if you've been married for a long time. The one where your spouse just cuts right through you.

I could see this wasn't fun and games. Did I struggle on through the full list?

Nope.

I got through three items.

For the next two and a half hours Carolyn laid into me and made me feel about an inch tall—like I'd never done anything right my whole married life. She just unloaded. Obviously, she was pretty frustrated with my behavior. I searched for something to say in response; the only thought that came to me was that I better just keep my mouth shut and listen. I didn't try to defend myself. I just tried to take it in quietly. When she was finally finished, I felt as if I'd been punched. . .knocked to my knees.

And here I was the person who was fixing to go out and challenge others.

My resolution to change allowed God to do something significant in my life. I began to do laundry, fix meals, do dishes—in short, I began to do a much, much better job *serving* Carolyn. I made a commitment to live this way every day, doing practical things to demonstrate my love for her. As a result, not only did my relationship with Carolyn change, but I also grew closer to the Lord. (After all, when we allow selfishness to come between others and us, it also puts us at a distance from Christ.) Through it all, my committed Christian friends helped hold me accountable. They helped me walk the daily path of discipleship. Carolyn, naturally, was the one who helped me most.

She came to me about four weeks later and said, "David, you are becoming a man of integrity—you are becoming a promise keeper." My heart soared. I'd never heard that, not from my father or anyone else close to me. But here was my wife of twenty-nine years, after just four weeks of my changed behavior, honoring me for my commitment. Her appreciation continued to replenish and refire my desire to serve her as Christ had called me.

This was a real turning point in our marriage. I had always felt we had a good marriage, but apparently, from her perspective, it had been a rotten marriage. After all, I never did anything. To this day, however, with thirty-plus years of marriage now behind us, I can look back and see the turnaround in our relationship.

My wife and I are many things to each other—but one of

these, certainly, is that we are fellow disciples who are there for one another; we disciple each other. The passage John 10:10 says, "The thief comes only to steal and kill and destroy; I have come that they may have life, and have it to the full." I feel that our marriage has gone from what was a mediocre marriage, at least in my wife's perception, to an abundant, full, and blessed one. My only wish is that I had done things differently from the very beginning instead of waiting until I'd been married for twenty-nine years. These days, one of my greatest joys is daily living a disciple's life alongside my bride.

I believe all of us benefit when we have people in our lives who can firmly say to us, "Hey, you need to change that behavior." Or, "I love you just the way you are—but Christ wants something more for you, something better. . .for us."

As I stated, I've become a zealot about walking individuals through a progression in their committed relationships, because I believe this is sorely needed in the body of Christ. We begin to see a whole different vision; we go from "you and me" (and I really don't care about "you") to "us." A truly committed, spiritual relationship goes far deeper than any other kind of friendship or acquaintance. As members of Christ's body here on earth, we really do need each other on a deep level.

SATAN'S PLAN

In chapter 2 I mentioned our failure to count the cost as one of the major obstacles to living the daily life of a disciple. Something else also eats like a cancer at our ability to pursue the disciple's life. It's called *isolation.*

In the Old Testament, take a look at what happened in 1 Samuel 11:11: "Saul separated his men into three divisions; during the last watch of the night they broke into the camp of the Ammonites and slaughtered them until the heat of the day. Those who survived were scattered, *so that no two of them were left together*" (emphasis added).

Satan's battle strategy is a lot like Saul's. In the area of committed, disciple-like relationships, Satan has sought to divide the body of Christ. It's a simple plan: First division, then separation, and then isolation. The end result is that you and I, joint members of Christ's body, feel as though we have no significant power or control over our own spiritual growth.

"But wait a minute," somebody says. "Jesus gave us power in the Spirit." This is correct, but if I don't realize this truth personally or have the vision of how to grow in Christ alongside others, then I *flounder* in my spiritual walk. On the other hand, however, if I see the vision and you see God's vision, then we can we affirm one another: "God's moving in your life. I can see it!" You know what that does in our spirits—it fires us up and affirms God's action in our lives.

The opposite of isolation is togetherness—biblical unity. Psalm 133:1 says, "How good and pleasant it is when brothers live together in unity!" In 1993 I was involved with a conference in Boulder, Colorado, where one of the main songs we sang during our worship times spoke of being *face-to-face, shoulder-to-shoulder, back-to-back,* with God and other Christians. The opposite of being isolated is to be shoulder to shoulder with one another. If you and I were out in the battlefield with our swords, defending ourselves against the Philistines, the Ammonites, the Moabites, or whoever is coming to attack us, we'd be guarding each other's backs. Our togetherness would give us protection from our enemies. There's great hope in that. Our faces are turned to God, seeking Him for direction, but we're shoulder-to-shoulder with each other. Together, we move forward under the momentum of the Spirit. That's a powerful symbolic picture.

FOR MEN, FOR WOMEN. . . FOR WOMEN, FOR MEN

E xperience and input has taught me that men and women experience relationships a little differently. Many women have no problem forming bonds of friendship with other women. Many men struggle to ever have a close friend.

For every relationship norm there is an exception, of course, and there are many books exploring the nuances (gender-based or otherwise) of relationships. For the purposes of this book, my primary concern is to inspire relationships that are committed to growth in Christ. At whatever level an individual is at in forming relationships, the point is, God intended for us to fully tap into the great resource He gave us in the rest of the body of Christ.

Are you not getting everything out of your current relationships? Do you feel something is still missing? Chances are some, if not all, of this chapter rings true for you. Satan, of course, tries to convince us that we're in the minority. (Whatever our struggle, he always tells us that we're the only one to experience it.) This, naturally, is a setup for his next trick: even deeper levels of isolation. Don't buy it. God wants something better for our lives. You're not alone. You're a part of a body, a body that needs you, a body that you need as well if you're to grow.

SERVING OTHERS

In an earlier chapter a key question was asked: What matters most in your life? Then a second: Have you ever made a difference in someone else's life?

One thing you might notice about these two questions is that an assumption has been made by the time we get to the second–the assumption that a person should *want* to make a difference in someone else's life. To some people in our world today this is a laughable premise. But I believe that our Creator breathed life into us for a purpose. We've been given an innate desire to make a difference in the world around us.

Some of you who are reading may still not be convinced, but take a look at Scripture. Whenever we're stuck in life we should always go back to Scripture (and if we spent more time there to begin with, perhaps we wouldn't get stuck nearly as often). Philippians 2:3–5 says this: "Do nothing out of selfish ambition or vain conceit, but in humility consider others better than yourselves. Each of you should look not only to your own interests, but also to the interests of others. Your attitude should be the same as that of Christ Jesus."

Of course, we're stuck if we haven't sought the mind of Christ in reaching out and serving others. There *has to be* a change in our attitude, one that reflects the spirit of this verse: "just as the Son of Man did not come to be served, but to serve. . ." (Matthew 20:28). Why is serving others so vital? Because committed relationships fall apart when they lack a serving attitude.

Servanthood goes against the grain of our society. Our natural tendencies follow a very different path. So where do we start? By asking God for help, by being vulnerable, by recognizing our need, and then by being willing to change, God will move; He can and will bring about a change in our hearts. Our Messiah says, "Narrow is the road." Not a lot of people are going to find this type of thing unless they are truly seeking. But I think down deep all of us genuinely want to make a difference in this life. The only way we'll do that is to focus on Christ's heart for serving others.

A profound change has occurred when a person is regenerated in Christ. Have we truly tapped into that change, though, and shifted away from pride, selfishness, ego, and a self-focus? God is saying that we need to be focused *on others* and what's going on in *their* lives. Let me say this again: Committed relationships fall apart aside from a servant focus–and living a disciple's life doesn't work without committed relationships.

A woman called Michele tells this story:

Growing up, I watched my mom acting like the family door-mat, and when I got married, I was determined I wouldn't let my husband walk all over me the way my mom had let my dad. Oh, I loved the guy–but that didn't mean that I was going to be his servant.

But as I've grown closer to Christ these last few years, not only has my heart changed, but my marriage has changed as well. I realized that if I'm truly following Jesus, then He wants me to look for ways to serve others–and that definitely includes my husband. That doesn't mean my husband gets to walk over me. Ideally, if he's following Jesus, too, it means he's busy serving me in return. But my job is to simply keep my eyes on Jesus, looking for all the little tangible ways I can demonstrate His love to those around me. Including my husband. If I'm Christ's disciple, I can't put myself first anymore. It's not always easy, but my husband and I are helping each other grow in this area. The change it's made in our relationship is unbelievable. I thought we had a good, stable marriage before—but it just keeps getting better.

Galatians 5:13 calls us to "serve one another in love." Typically, we don't see an instant transition where I move from self-focus to focusing on others. This sort of change does not come quickly or easily. It requires self-discipline. It requires a whole new mindset. As Michele discovered, change like this is difficult *at best*. We aren't particularly naturally predisposed to being good candidates for this. But the burden was never meant to be carried alone. When we labor together, even the hardest work becomes a little easier.

MENTALITY OF THE WORLD

Christians all around us have read through the Philippians 2:3–5 and Galatians 5:13 verses and allowed the words to bounce right off them. Why? What is it that the floundering believer buys into? I call it "the Wall Street" mentality. It's so American. We're bombarded every day with countless media images that say "go for the gusto" or "you can do it all." I'm amused by the title of one of the books the business world puts out: *Gorilla Tactics.* People are, for the most part, "looking out for number one." If I'm young or immature in Christ, I'm often bombarded with this kind of thinking every day; inevitably it becomes part of my lifestyle. In a recent survey, when Christian school students were asked "What constitutes success?" the following answers were some of the top responses: win the lottery, think of a great product and sell a million of them, become a rock star, become a famous actor, get into professional sports, or get into the stock market.[4] Popular culture teaches that we all have to accomplish various things in order to be deemed successful.

As we get older or more mature in Christ, we realize that "the American dream" wasn't really true. . .it didn't really work out like we thought. We've seen the bumper stickers that say, "He who dies with the most toys wins." But in the end it's all just going to be dust! The people we've invested in are the only thing that will matter. Serving others is what counts.

There is one advantage to age or maturity, and that is experience. You can look back and say, "This worked, and this didn't work." Both in a spiritual sense and in a practical, life sense. There's a little saying that says, "If only youth knew, if only old age could." Ideally if youth *knew* and had the experience, they wouldn't make the same mistakes. They wouldn't be focused on the wrong areas. If old age only *could* do what youth do with their exuberance and energy, there's little they couldn't accomplish. People may learn too late about the value of serving.

SPENDING TIME WITH OTHERS

I f we're obsessed with the agenda that comes with the Wall Street mentality, we have little room in our lives for committed relationships where spiritual growth can occur. But as

Christians, things are supposed to be different with us. We need to drop the self-focused agenda of the world. Look at what Jesus—our Savior and example in everything—did while He was here on earth. Take to heart the following quote from Dr. Richard Halverson in the book *Bonds of Iron*:

> *One of the decisive texts for my ministry was given to me in the early 1940s when I was clearly being led into a discipling ministry. . . . There were no books being published on this back then, so I decided to read the gospels and find out how Jesus did what He did. As I read about Jesus as He met and dealt with people, I began to realize that there was no clear "how to" with these encounters. Every encounter was different because everyone He met was different. Then I realized that He didn't have an agenda. What determined the agenda of each encounter was the need of the person. Love responding to the need determined the agenda.*
>
> *Mark in his Gospel talks about Jesus selecting His disciples. Mark says it in a very interesting way: "Jesus appointed the twelve—ordaining them apostles—that they might be with him and that he might send them out to preach" (Mark 3:14). The most important word in that text for me was the word* with. *The only way you can disciple people is to be with people.*[5]

THE VALUE OF CLOSE FRIENDS

The third key question I asked you earlier was: Do you have a close friend (one who loves you, but is not impressed by you)?

Some of us tend not to have had a best friend since high school. Even fewer have a Proverbs 17:17 friend.

As we begin our careers and families, we can literally become isolated from developing close friends. ("But the worries of this life and the deceitfulness of wealth choke it, making it unfruitful." Matthew 13:22) And yet we all need a close friend who, as Howard Hendricks would say, "loves you but is not impressed by you." This is the epitome of the Proverbs 17:17 friend: one who loves us at all times and who is there for us in times of adversity. This is a person who "holds our feet to the fire" when it comes to making the right spiritual choices.

Daily we are confronted with decisions; some are simply procedural or functional, while other choices can drastically change our lives, positively or negatively. When we lack a close friend, someone to whom we can be accountable, we teeter on the brink of a meltdown. Worse, when we do not have a "2 A.M." friend (one who would drop what he is doing at any time in order to meet our need), I believe we allow ourselves to miss out on God's provision for our lives. God uses other people to touch us. . .to bring us His love and His direction.

Once we have gotten too busy with work or career—or anything else that keeps us from experiencing the love of God through others—we usually run into division of some kind. We are then *divided* from a critical spiritual/relational base that God intended for us. Finally we may become *isolated* and potentially ineffective spiritually. Satan's plan for individual destruction is realized when a man or woman is isolated from the fellowship of other Christians. (Remember, "Those who survived were scattered, so that no two of them were left together." 1 Samuel 11:11)

Yet a vital point to remember is this: *We can have great victory over our adversary the devil when we intentionally seek out and develop spiritual relationships where we are committed to be there for one another.*

A biblical model of this covenant comes from the relationship of Jonathan and David, found in 1 Samuel 20:16–17: "So Jonathan made a covenant with the house of David, saying, 'May the LORD call David's enemies to account.' And Jonathan had David reaffirm his oath out of love for him, because he loved him as he loved himself."

Please don't misunderstand what I am advocating here—it's not about oath-taking, it's about *committing ourselves to our relationships.*

Living a disciple's daily life means reaching out and becoming a close friend to another; it means finding another who will commit with you to "stick closer than" a brother or a sister (Proverbs 18:24). It doesn't matter who initiates the relationship; what matters is that the relationship is developed "to equip the saints for the work of ministry, for building up the body of Christ" (Ephesians 4:12 NRSV).

Do *you* have a close friend, committed to walking alongside you as you grow together in Christ? If not, what can you do about it? Take a step in the right direction today.

APPLICATIONS TO DAILY LIFE

1. Has a close relationship ever challenged you to change? In what ways? How did you feel about this at the time? How do you feel about it now? Are you open today to being challenged by the people with whom you have committed relationships?

2. Do you focus on others? Think of someone with whom you have a close relationship. What practical ways can you serve him or her?

CHAPTER 4

Mentoring and Discipleship

Teach the older women. . . .
Then they can train the younger women. . . .
TITUS 2:3–4

A s we talk about these committed relationships, you may
be wondering: What do they look like? What's the difference between different kinds of relationships? Is simple friendship different from discipleship? Is discipleship the same as
mentoring?

I define an acquaintance as simply somebody with whom I
am familiar. A person I have met. The acquaintance stage can
develop into friendship through spending time together,
through opening ourselves up and being transparent. As I reveal who I am to you, as I make myself vulnerable, as you do
the same, we can begin to develop trust between us. With this
trust as the foundation of our relationship, we can even go so
far as to give one another permission to ask tough questions, to
challenge each other in certain areas when we need it, to tell
each other the truth about what we're really like.

After time, we can reach a stage where we have developed
a truly committed relationship–I call this brotherhood or sisterhood. An acquaintance is someone I know about. A friend is
someone I am working to know better and better over time. A
brother or sister is someone I know *personally*. Honestly, I
would have to admit that I'm probably not too quick to risk

everything for an acquaintance. But I would be willing to die for a brother or sister. We're that closely knit. In 1 Samuel 18:3 we read, "And Jonathan made a covenant with David because he loved him as himself." When I've just begun to know someone, I wouldn't expect something like the David-Jonathan friendship—or the Naomi-Ruth relationship mentioned earlier—but eventually, when we are mutually committed to each other, this sort of deep relationship does grow.

As we move forward in our relationships with others and closer to the brotherhood or sisterhood stage, an interesting thing happens. We become closer to the model Jesus gave us for committed relationships—and together, day by day, we begin to follow the biblical models for a disciple's life. (However, please understand that I am not an advocate of deeply personal relationships between married men and women with members of the opposite sex other than their spouses.)

THE ECCLESIASTES 4:12 MODEL

At a conference I attended some years ago, Howard Hendricks mentioned a great relationship model. I call it the Ecclesiastes 4:12 model—"A cord of three strands is not quickly broken." This model explains three kinds of relationships we all need in our lives as disciples.

First, we each need a mentor—an older person (or one who is more mature in Christ). Second, we need an encouragement/accountability partner, a fellow disciple who is an equal with us. And last, we should each invest in the life of a younger person (or one who is less mature in Christ). When I use this model to look back on my life, I realize that half a decade ago I had zero mentors, no encouragement/accountability partners, and about five younger Christians with whom I was working. Today I have three mentors, five encouragement/accountability partners, and about the same number of younger Christians with whom I'm spending time investing my life.

Occasionally you may start out knowing an individual in one kind of relationship role, but then the relationship may change to a different "strand" of the cord. An older gentleman named Cliff Martin, a man who demonstrates great wisdom, was initially my encouragement/accountability partner, but now he's a mentor. This man loves me, and he is concerned about my walk with the Lord and how I treat my wife and family. He has permission from me to ask tough questions when necessary to challenge my thinking on issues. This is not a role he is shy about. In fact, sometimes I wonder if he doesn't relish it just a bit from time to time.

CONFRONTED

One day Cliff took a look at my appointment calendar and said, "Dave, let me ask you a question here. Your ministry has a policy that a person should only be out traveling a maximum of ten days a month—but I'm looking across your schedule and I'm counting up twenty-two days that you're away from home every month. Now your employer has said *ten* days and you're trying to do twenty-two. You obviously have an ego problem. Why are you doing this?"

You can probably imagine my reaction. I began to hem and

haw—but he cut me off.

"From my perspective, comparing your schedule to your ministry's policy, I feel you've lied to me. You're a liar," he said.

This, coming from my friend!

My jaw went tight and my neck felt hot and I said something like, "No, you don't understand. . .I'm doing God's work."

Cliff wasn't buying it. He looked at me and said, "No."

I had no excuse. He was right. And by being confronted face to face with the truth, I was jarred back to reality.

Cliff's words opened my eyes. We went on to a calmer dialogue about *why* I was acting the way I had been—and how I could change to become a better servant. Ultimately, I realized something clearly: I was ignoring my wife by being away all the time—even in the name of Christian work. (We always try to rationalize things, don't we?) The good that came out of this incident was that I had another meaningful talk with my wife; she agreed that I'd been gone too often, and the next month I managed to cut my travel days down from twenty-two to eleven.

One of the key elements of this incident with Cliff was the closeness and trust he and I had developed over time. That relationship is what allowed him to approach me in the manner he did, because he not only knew *what* I needed to hear, he also knew *me* well enough to understand how I needed to hear it. I'm convinced that every person needs someone who knows them well and offers them regular encouragement—but also loves them enough to challenge them and ask tough questions when they are warranted. This obviously doesn't mean, though, that when we start up a new friendship, we levy all sorts of criticism against the other person based on our own personal convictions. But when a solid relationship built on trust has been established, then this part of the disciple's life can take place.

Daily DISCIPLES

An author I'll call Louise tells of a similar mentoring relationship in her own life:

I had always felt God calling me to write, ever since I was very young. My aunt Mari was my mentor, someone who encouraged me every step of the way. She taught me all that she knew, and cheered me on as my career grew. She helped me dedicate to God this gift I've been given.

Lately, though, my focus had become confused. My career had grown, and I'd been presented with lots of opportunities, opportunities to make more money than I ever had before, but somehow a lot of the joy had gotten lost along the way. Instead of feeling excited and inspired by my work, the way I used to, I'd been feeling simply overwhelmed and pressured.

I'm so grateful that Aunt Mari loved me enough to sit me down and get me to talk out all my confusion and exhaustion. When I was done, she asked me gently, "Where is Jesus in all of this?"

"Well. . .I. . .I guess. . ." But I couldn't answer her. I didn't know where Jesus was in my career. Where once He'd been my leader each step of the way, somewhere along the way I'd lost sight of His face.

"What does that tell you about the work you're doing now?" Aunt Mari asked me.

My face got hot, but I knew she was right. No matter how much money I was making, none of it meant anything if I wasn't serving Jesus with my writing. I needed to reexamine my priorities; I needed to put Him first in my career once more.

Once I did, everything began to change. But if Aunt Mari hadn't loved me enough to help me find my path again, I probably would have spent months, probably even years, stumbling along getting more and more lost.

We all need strong mentors like this in our lives. And we need to be willing to be mentors to those less experienced than ourselves, so that those coming after us will also have someone to help them find their path. As I mentioned earlier, however, I don't believe Christians should be legalistic when they challenge each other on various things. This is an important point to always keep in mind as we disciple one another. Romans 14 deals in depth with this very principle; no Christian is the ultimate judge of anyone, and we certainly shouldn't act like we are. Romans 14:5, 7–8 says,

> *One man considers one day more sacred than another; another man considers every day alike. Each one should be fully convinced in his own mind. . . . For none of us lives to himself alone and none of us dies to himself alone. If we live, we live to the Lord; and if we die, we die to the Lord. So, whether we live or die, we belong to the Lord.*

We are often very different, yet we serve the same God. I believe God has given me a special passion for the disciple's life—but another person may feel a special calling for evangelism, or overseas mission work, or something else. We all have special gifts and different passions we can use to build up the body of Christ. These gifts and passions should always be balanced with respect for another's call from the Lord.

When should we forgo acceptance and pursue confrontation? This is a sensitive issue. I believe we must first always develop a relationship with the other person, over time, which allows the individual to get to know and respect us. When we mutually confide in each other, we have the common ground to see into (and when necessary, probe into) one another's issues and lives. Ultimately, if we are wise, we always approach issues in the spirit of love, because "love covers over a multitude of sins" (1 Peter 4:8).

Committed love always wants the best for the other person. Sometimes that means we need to speak some difficult truths rather than simply stroke each other's egos. Jesus certainly challenged His disciples when they needed it—and they didn't always like it. I didn't like it when my wife and Cliff confronted me. But when a person has the courage to challenge us in love, we need to respond in love, regardless of our level of agreement or lack thereof. This is what takes place in a committed relationship.

Seeking Counsel

Many well-meaning people may have a simple lack of knowledge about how to form committed relationships, whether beginning one or taking an already-existing friendship to a deeper spiritual level. In many cases people don't know how to reach out to someone, either to be discipled or to disciple them. Very few are usually bold enough to simply ask. Consequently, we have countless members of the body of Christ who are floundering spiritually. We are in spiritual neutral. We're not going anywhere.

If you were to go skiing in the mountains and had never done it before, you could rent skis, you could buy skis, get all the necessary equipment, buy your lift ticket, and you could get out on the slope and try to ski. But what's the problem with that? Without proper instruction, you're going to get hurt.

What would be the wise thing to do? Take lessons from a qualified instructor. Be patient. Take a season or two to learn, and then ski well. Some individuals I know just go up and get their skis, jump on the slope, and then they come back to work on Monday with a cast on. And then you hear stuff like, "This thing hurts. I'm not going to do this anymore." In the same way, we have Christians who say, "Been there, done that. I tried the small group relationship thing and it didn't 'do it' for me." What they are really saying is, "I'm not going to attempt again and again to get into a vital spiritual relationship, because it didn't work before. It's a lot less dangerous to just avoid it, and I don't want to be let down or rejected again."

Whether learning to ski or seeking spiritual growth, we must seek expert instruction. In the Christian world, where do we find this wise instruction? Jesus said, "The harvest is plentiful but the workers are few. Ask the Lord of the harvest, therefore, to send out workers into his harvest field" (Matthew 9:37–38). I believe that anyone can experience committed relationships if they are willing to seek after God with all their hearts (Psalm 119:10), and ask Him to be their guide as they seek others to be part of their lives.

I think of the time when I took one of my sons out to learn how to water-ski. Shame on me, because we were using an underpowered boat and I stuck him out there in cold water. Consequently, he couldn't even get up and we were dragging him along. . . "Gee, thanks, Dad." If I would've put him in a wet suit to keep him warm and put him behind a fast boat, he could've gotten up and skied right away. His experience would have been positive and he might have loved waterskiing. But my son, like some of us in relationships, ended up having a negative experience.

The first time I ever water skied I had a professional instructor behind me holding me up, shouting directions in my ear. I even slalom-skied alone my first time, due to expert instruction. Men and women need to understand this principle. Seek wise counsel! You may have to spend some time looking for it—but it's well worth the effort.

A WORD ABOUT MENTORING AND DISCIPLESHIP

Mentoring is a part (a very important one) of the overall process of living a disciple's life. As I just explained, we all need wise counsel. While I feel strongly that seeking this counsel is valuable, we also need to keep things in proper perspective and not allow a power imbalance to occur. As disciples we must always interact first and foremost with God; our interactions with each other ought never to serve as a substitute for that.

Allow me to illustrate. A woman I'll call Nancy shared with me this story:

I've been mentored twice in my life, both times by older women. The first woman I met when I was in my early twenties, and at that time she made a tremendous difference in my life spiritually. But twenty years later, I find myself in an uncomfortable position with her, in that I've outgrown her spiritually, and yet she still seeks to direct my actions and spiritual life. She's hurt if I don't still turn to her for counsel—but I feel more and more that her advice simply confuses me and gets me off track from where God would want me to go. My other experience of being mentored currently seems far healthier—the bottom line for this woman is always simply: "What would Christ have you to do? What decision will lead you closer to Him? Is this an issue you really need to talk more about—or at this point do you need to simply pray about it?"

Nancy also has known another area where mentoring relationships can become unhealthy. She shared, "As a woman who mentors other women as well, I also have experienced the temptation from the other side. I want to 'fix' everything for the other person. Sometimes I long to get in there and make things right. Often I need to be reminded that the best thing I can do for my friend is simply pray and leave her in God's hands. We are not God, and we do not have all the answers, nor can we fix everything."

Many men I have encountered also struggle with a tendency to "fix." Obviously, this desire isn't evil by itself—but if we allow it to become our answer to everything, we can easily miss what God might be saying. And, as Nancy's story illustrates, some relationships can take a turn for the worse if individuals want to "fix" us or seemingly have their identity wrapped up in directing our paths.

Fortunately, my initial experience with mentoring was a positive one. And, in fact, I believe most mentoring relationships are healthy or they can be. The question we must always come back to is this: What would Jesus want me to do? Am I growing closer to Him or away from Him? That is the standard against which all our relationships must be judged.

Over twenty years ago, I was blessed when the church we were in assigned my wife and me a couple who came alongside us as we became new members. Not everyone has this going for them. In fact, most churches don't do this kind of thing. What this couple did was lead us and provide a positive disciple's model for three years, similar to the model Jesus demonstrated for all.

Many, many of us in the body of Christ have tender hearts and a desire to do the will of our Father in heaven—but we have no direction, no vision. One way we develop this sense of direction is from reading the Bible, and later I will discuss this more. The other part of the answer to this problem, however, is that we should not attempt to "get this Christian life right" out on our own. Even knowing that we will always face risks in any human (therefore never infallible) relationship, we simply cannot afford to become isolated. Isolation is the result of either outright relationship avoidance or resistance to God's voice telling us to pursue something deeper for already-existing relationships. The outcome of either is typically worse than the risks we face in relationships.

The critic might say, "Well, ignorance breeds ignorance. What if the person I form a relationship with just gets me more confused than ever?" This may be true in some cases, such as the first mentoring relationship Nancy described. Human beings do let us down; after all they're only human, and only God is perfect. But in Ecclesiastes 4:9 we are told, "Two are better than one." And then later the verse we've already mentioned, "A cord of three strands is not quickly broken" (4:12). This is true on a human level, as the author of Ecclesiastes understood—and it is certainly true as well on a spiritual level.

STEPS IN THE JOURNEY

M entoring relationships are one important way we can go deeper as daily disciples. As we begin to grow toward maturity in our spiritual journey, we will also spend more time in the Word, more time in prayer, more time in all of our committed relationships. God in His infinite wisdom slowly begins to reveal to us through revelation, *literally* spiritual revelation, what we are to be doing—His purposes for our life. When we grow more mature in Christ, we understand our spiritual journey is a process of successive steps. The sad part of it is that many of us are still babes in the faith (1 Peter 2:2). We've not moved on from spiritual milk to the real meat of maturity in Christ. Maybe we don't know how. We haven't searched the Scriptures. We don't have people in our lives who are showing us the way toward Christlike change, nor are we reaching out to others.

If this is true for you, then a change is needed in your life. Chances are if you've read this far, you *have* felt that sense deep down that something isn't right. Chances are you are wanting to take that next step. Be encouraged! You are not alone! If you're a daily disciple, you will progressively, step-by-step, grow toward spiritual maturity.

It's time, then, to develop a personal vision for living as a daily disciple.

APPLICATIONS TO DAILY LIFE

1. Do you know someone who is more experienced spiritually than you? How can you learn from that person's life? How do you think that person would react if you sought him out as a mentor, whether formally or informally?

2. Do you know someone who is less experienced spiritually than yourself? Are you aware of your power to influence this person's life? Can you think of any concrete ways you could encourage this person on his or her spiritual journey?

CHAPTER 5

The Word
(and Your Vision)

Where there is no vision,
the people are unrestrained.
PROVERBS 29:18 NASB

A s we've already said, the Word is an important element in
the life of a disciple. In this chapter, we're going to look
at how the Bible can help us develop a personal vision for being a daily disciple.

Most Christian people can see–but do they have vision?
Obviously, there's a major difference between having eyesight
and having a spiritual vision for our lives. The Word of God is
talking about a sense of spiritual direction in Proverbs 29:18.

How are we going to stay on that narrow path that Christ
mentioned in the Book of Matthew? I don't think we can if we
lack a sense of spiritual direction. Our life as a Christian is a
journey toward Christlikeness. Having a personal vision is
what starts us and sustains us along the road.

So what is a personal vision? The way I would define it is
this: *trying to see as God sees.* We need to have God impart, into
our own minds, His vision. When the Lord casts a vision for
our lives, we must receive that vision and step out in faith:

When you come to the edge of all the light you have known
and are about to step out into darkness, faith is knowing one
of two things will happen. There will be something to stand
on, or you will be taught how to fly. ANONYMOUS

HELPING EACH OTHER SEE

I f a friend of mine and I were blindfolded and we approached an elephant from different sides, you can imagine the different impressions we'd get. My friend feels a leg, and I grab the trunk. We would very likely draw different conclusions about what an elephant is like. Now if we take the blindfolds off, we can see the entire elephant, the total picture. There's a lot more to the whole than we'd realized. In the spiritual life, we know that we need to take one thing at a time; master one part of the elephant before we assume we've conquered the whole. It certainly helps to be able to see the entire mass of the elephant!

The immature Christian walks up to the elephant of personal spiritual growth, feels the leg, and to her that's all there is. She may think spiritual life is all about reading the Bible; she assumes that's the only thing she needs to grow as a Christian. Yet another person, however, may think the life of a Christian is simply about "being nice"; he believes that getting along with everyone, forming relationships with others, is what makes a good Christian. Still yet another individual may perceive that spiritual growth is simply about being "moral" enough to tell other people what to do. And growing as a Christian may mean something else entirely to you.

Far too many of us see just a small, small piece of the whole, and then we assume that that's all there is to Christianity. That's one reason why we need to be willing to listen and learn from one another, so that we can benefit from each other's perspectives. That's the only way we can ever hope to catch even a glimpse of the whole "elephant." The truth is, being a daily disciple is deep, rich life that contains many factors. But again, without a vision, we aren't going to get anywhere substantial in our Christian life.

VISION FOR THE ROAD AHEAD

Most businesses these days develop a vision statement that gives their organization direction and purpose. I believe every individual also needs a personal vision for his or her life. My wife Carolyn and I have a vision for our marriage we've drawn from Galatians 6:2: "Carry each other's burdens, and in this way you will fulfill the law of Christ." A few of the ways in which I've carried out this vision for our marriage is by doing very concrete tasks—like doing the dishes, washing laundry, and fixing dinner.

Some people are uncomfortable with the word "vision." They think *vision* is synonymous with *prophecy*. So then, if someone talks about having a vision from God, they say, "Who do you think you are, some sort of modern-day prophet?" But this is not what I am talking about here. Using the Word to give us a personal vision to direct our lives is a *biblical* idea. We are not trying to add teachings to what has already been revealed through the Bible. Instead, we are trying to keep our eyes focused on God so we can finish the task before us as we grow to maturity in Christ. I'm not talking here about concocting our own vision; rather, I'm saying we should take ownership of His vision for us and make it our personal responsibility.

Sometimes your vision may be as simple as the answer to the question, "What is it that you want to do?" What is it you hope to achieve, both in your personal walk with God and in the Church?

Do *you* have a vision as it relates to God's will in your life?

AIMING AT NOTHING

Our vision can be applied wherever we are. In our church, in our small group, with another ministry. In all of these arenas, what do we want to do?

Perhaps what we want most is to evangelize others. Well, we must define, then, how evangelizing others is going to happen. What does evangelization look like? What's our plan? What is our strategy? We aren't going to arrive at the right place simply through osmosis. As the saying goes, when we aim at *nothing* we tend to hit it every time. This is where a relationship with other Christians can help us in our walk as daily disciples. These trusted individuals in our lives can help us hammer out our vision and then hold us accountable to its claim on our lives.

Christ gave us an example of what having a vision means. He said in John 8:14, " 'I know where I came from and where I am going.' " And in John 17, He talks more about His vision for Himself, as well as His vision for the disciples and for all believers. In fact, all of John 17 is an excellent discourse on Jesus' vision from God for us. Take a look at these verses (20–23):

"My prayer is not for them alone. I pray also for those who will believe in me through their message, that all of them may be one, Father, just as you are in me and I am in you. May they also be in us so that the world may believe that you have sent me. I have given them the glory that you gave me, that they

may be one as we are one: I am in them and you in me. May
they be brought to complete unity to let the world know that
you sent me and have loved them even as you have loved me."

THE ENEMY'S DECEPTION

This was Jesus' prayer for us all, but Satan wants to do all
that he can to keep it from happening. That's why he lies
to us, convincing many of us that there is something about us
that will always keep us from having a clear direction in our
lives. The devil delights in seeing Christians without any type
of vision for what they want to do. As in the verse that preludes
this chapter, the visionless, "unrestrained" person is someone
Satan has no reason to fear. The King James Bible translates
Proverbs 29:18 this way: "Where there is no vision, the people
perish." We know that the enemy wants nothing less than to
destroy us; no wonder, a lack of vision must look pretty good
to him. Our adversary wants to keep us from ever even trying
to find God's vision for us, let alone pursuing it with zeal. Sadly,
this plan succeeds all too often throughout the body of Christ.

Many believers simply do not know what to do. But the
truth is, if we study the plan laid out for us in the Bible, we'll
see that God doesn't want us to wander aimlessly through life.
James 1:5–6 tells us, "If any of you lacks wisdom, he should ask
God, who gives generously to all without finding fault, and it
will be given to him. But when he asks, he must believe and not
doubt, because he who doubts is like a wave of the sea, blown
and tossed by the wind."

It's time for us to stop being tossed by the wind. As we ask for and seek His vision for our lives through the Word, we then must step out in faith to allow the Holy Spirit to begin His work. God *will* honor our efforts.

FORMULATING A VISION STATEMENT

W here I work we have a very clear vision that's posted up on the wall. Our vision is to see a vibrant men's ministry in every Bible-believing, Christ-centered, servant-oriented church in America, and to have a vital prayer partnership with each of those churches. Most Christian ministries, magazines, or publishers have a statement of some kind that enunciates their vision. If you were to ask the question of each, "What are you trying to do?" the answer would be found in their vision statement.

Some people, if you were to talk to them about a personal vision, would claim not to have one. Probably, though, they do have a vision for themselves of some kind. Perhaps they are not aware that it is there, or they haven't identified it as a personal vision, but still something directs the direction of their lives. They may have a recreational vision of some great glorious achievement they want to attain in a sport—or a career vision of becoming a CEO someday—or a domestic vision for what they want their married or home life to be like, and so on. Something is driving us.

What is it that you want to do? If you have no answer for that question, then you aren't driven to do much. Yet most people are motivated to achieve. It's one of the things that's a part of the American way. Most people just take it for granted. Their answer to this question may be a subconscious thing, but something drives them.

As Christians we need to be more clear about what motivates us. Living daily as a disciple isn't going to happen if we don't have a personal vision from the Word. If you asked the question, "Do you want to be like Jesus?" my assumption is that most believers would answer a resounding "Yes!" But Christlikeness doesn't happen by itself. It won't happen if we never think about how we are going to make it happen.

While there is nothing magical about having words on a piece of paper, there *is* something significant about taking the time to think through what you are trying to accomplish, so it can then be put into a statement of some kind. In our ministries at the church, do we have a vision? Do people know what it is? Do the teachers and leaders know? What about the participants? Has the vision ever been written out or communicated in some fashion? Do we have a vision for the children's Sunday school program? Again, has the vision ever been shared among the people responsible for making it happen?

All these questions apply to our personal lives as well. Who are we? Where are we going? How are we going to get there? In our lives outside of the local church, what is our vision? What are we trying to accomplish? A vision must be shaped before it can be acted upon. We wouldn't think of trying to catch a fish on a new lure without ever casting the thing into the water. Yet, in our churches and in our lives we often try to get by without ever establishing a firm direction.

Daily DISCIPLES

OUR LIVES' FOUNDATION

For the first thirty years of Christ's life, He had no public ministry; after that, His public ministry began and flourished (to say the least). How can we learn from His example?

Our vision can be personal enough that it doesn't have to be something we advertise. Or perhaps we share our vision with others in the hope that they will catch on to it, too. Either way, we are all accountable to God first and foremost. Our personal vision may be something that is misunderstood by others. If we look at Jesus, it becomes quickly apparent that having an eternal focus makes no sense in worldly terms. But that doesn't matter if we're trying to see as God sees.

The Apostle Paul spoke of the foundation we all need to seek as Christians:

By the grace God has given me, I laid a foundation as an expert builder, and someone else is building on it. But each one should be careful how he builds. For no one can lay any foundation other than the one already laid, which is Jesus Christ. If any man builds on this foundation using gold, silver, costly stones, wood, hay or straw, his work will be shown for what it is, because the Day will bring it to light. It will be revealed with fire, and the fire will test the quality of each man's work. If what he has built survives, he will receive his reward. 1 CORINTHIANS 3:10–14

Christ is our strong foundation. Too many Christians, however, lose hope when they don't get instant mature Christianity. Don't buy into that. Keep building patiently on the foundation.

94

It's got to be a process.

But the process needs to start with a personal vision—one that's gleaned from the Word.

THE BIRTH OF YOUR VISION

I f you haven't ever developed a personal vision for living daily as a disciple, today is your day to start. Oswald Chambers said:

> *Every vision will be made real if we will have patience.*
> *Think of the enormous leisure of God! He is never in a hurry.*
> *We are always in such a frantic hurry. In the light of the*
> *glory of the vision we go forth to do things, but the vision is*
> *not real in us yet; and God has to take us into the valley, and*
> *put us through fires and floods to batter us into shape, until*
> *we get to the place where He can trust us with the veritable*
> *reality.*[1]

Let me help you establish a plan of action to accomplish your vision. Some of you may be thinking, "Give me a successful plan of action that will give direction to my life, and I will be satisfied." Well, I can give you points for action or an outline or strategy, but let me ask you this: What is God's vision for your life and how do you find that out?

Simple: Ask Him! Continue to ask Him and wait upon Him until you receive an answer. The Bible says, "Yet those who wait for the LORD will gain new strength; they will mount up with wings like eagles, they will run and not get tired, they will walk and not become weary" (Isaiah 40:31 NASB).

I also recommend prayer and fasting. I would even suggest reading the entire Book of Ecclesiastes over and over. When saturated, read the Book of Proverbs over and over. When saturated, read the Book of Psalms over and over. Shut off the television. You have too much reading you need to be doing. Get off the Internet. . . . Get the picture? You need to shut off the world's voice so you can hear God's.

If you still are having trouble developing a vision for your life (let alone putting some type of plan into action), let me suggest a simple plan to get started. Keep this in mind: If you can consciously repeat something thirty days in a row, it will become a habit and part of your daily routine. This applies to prayer, Bible study, or any other area you want to make a consistent habit.

Helen Keller said, "Is there anything worse than blindness? Oh, yes! A person with sight and no vision."[2]

APPLICATIONS TO DAILY LIFE

Review the six questions from chapter 2 to set the tone for your strategy. Now answer these questions as well:

1. Given that what will matter most in eternity are people and relationships, who are the people in my life I should be working to know better?

2. What brings me the greatest joy? What makes me laugh?

3. What legacy have I invested in that cannot be destroyed and will last for eternity?

4. Do I have a short-term plan and a long-term plan that will lead to personal spiritual growth (such as a planned study)?

5. What spiritual gifts do I have that would enhance my vision? (See Spiritual Gifts Inventory in Appendix A.)

6. What realistic changes can I attempt to make right now? Who will help me or hold me accountable to make these changes right now?

7. Have I evaluated my life realistically to see if I am moving toward God or away from Him?

As you consider these questions, make note of factors that come to your mind that can move your vision to reality. Now, with your heart and mind being challenged to answer some practical questions to accomplish your vision, begin to meditate upon and claim for yourself Romans 8:26–27:

> *The Spirit helps us in our weakness. We do not know what we ought to pray for, but the Spirit himself intercedes for us with groans that words cannot express. And he who searches our hearts knows the mind of the Spirit, because the Spirit intercedes for the saints in accordance with God's will.*

Here is a final note of encouragement, again from Oswald Chambers, to bear in mind as you proceed:

The vision is not a castle in the air, but a vision of what God wants you to be. Let Him put you on His wheel and whirl you as He likes, and as sure as God is God and you are you, you will turn out exactly in accordance with the vision. Don't lose heart in the process.[3]

The vision is there for your taking!

CHAPTER 6

Prayer

I said a prayer for you today
And know God must have heard;
I felt the answer in my heart
Although He spoke not a word.
I didn't ask for wealth or fame
(I knew you wouldn't mind):
I asked for priceless treasures rare
of a more lasting kind.
I prayed that He'd be near to you
At the start of each new day,
To grant you health and blessings fair,
And friends to share your way.
I asked for happiness for you
In all things great and small,
But that you'd know His loving care
I prayed the most of all.

ANONYMOUS

A nyone can pray. In fact, nine out of ten Americans say they pray—75 percent say they *pray daily.*[1]

Prayer isn't a hidden talent. All it takes is a willingness to spend the time to do it. In the daily disciple's life, prayer is a core element that holds the other pieces together.

Statistics indicate most people "get" the idea of prayer (at least on a basic level), and this book will not be spending a great amount of time on the subject. I believe, however, we need to cover at least a few important points in regard to prayer as we develop a life of daily discipleship.

Although nearly everyone says they pray, few people understand the magnitude and power of prayer. Too many Christians pray only for personal needs and wants, while they miss out on the joy of simply communicating with the Father, Jesus, and the Holy Spirit. The wise person, however, understands that prayer is the key to opening the door to God's heart.

Prayer is a simple concept and yet profound. It does not require a special language, but it does require time, effort, and a willingness to listen for God's "still small voice." To be a friend of God and spend time with Him, we must learn to listen to God as well as to make requests of Him. He *has* given us permission to ask Him for our needs and wants (Matthew 7:7–8, John 15:7), and most of us don't have a hard time asking. Usually, though, the most difficult part of prayer is to be still and listen to God (Psalm 46:10).

This requires an intentional effort to eliminate what could hinder us. We must set aside a specific time and place for in-depth prayer–away from the television, computer, hobbies, and other distractions (Matthew 6:6). That time could be in the morning–a commitment that many I know make–or at some other point throughout the day. Of course, what's important is not so much *when* you pray, but that you do pray.

Personally, I enjoy exercise in the morning, but I've had to discipline myself to spend time with God first. I developed a saying for myself: "No Word, no workout!" You may not feel the same attraction to exercise that I do–but imagine if people had the philosophy of "No prayer, no sleep!" or "No prayer, no meals!" This may sound extreme, but everyone I talk with struggles with a specific commitment to prayer time on a daily basis. And yet no matter how busy our days, we all make time for a daily shower, meals, and at least some sleep. We need to see prayer as the same kind of priority in our lives.

Some people have found that keeping a prayer journal helps

them remain focused while they pray, and it also provides them with a way to chronicle their requests and God's answers.

Whatever method works best for you, Scripture makes clear that God's will for us is to "pray continually" (1 Thessalonians 5:17). This means that we have a constant *attitude* of prayer; whatever specific daily prayer habits work for us, we all need to have our hearts constantly open to God, even in the midst of our most hectic moments.

THE PRAYER LIFE OF CHRIST

J esus modeled a consistent, committed prayer life. He was aware that He could do nothing but what the Father did through Him (John 5:19). That's why Jesus sought His Father's counsel at all times of the day or night (Mark 1:35, Luke 6:12) and in all circumstances. He taught His disciples how to pray in Matthew 6:5–15, including what is now known as "The Lord's Prayer."

"Our Father in heaven, hallowed be your name, your kingdom come, your will be done on earth as it is in heaven. Give us today our daily bread. Forgive us our debts, as we also have forgiven our debtors. And lead us not into temptation, but deliver us from the evil one."

Jesus realized He was at war with the spiritual forces of evil, and He recognized prayer as His number-one defense against the attacks of Satan. We need that same understanding in our own lives (Ephesians 6:12).

Many people have heard of "The Lord's Prayer." Fewer know that it was offered by Jesus in response to this inquiry from one of His disciples: *"Lord, teach us to pray."*

This leads to an important question. What if we're stuck in our prayer lives? Or what if we don't know where to start? My suggestion: Pray about your prayer life. Say to God, *"Lord, teach me how to pray."* If we learn anything from the Bible, we know Christ will honor our efforts if we seek Him with our heart and mind.

ONE WOMAN'S COMMITMENT TO PRAYER

In the Gospel of Luke, an individual is briefly mentioned, whose entire legacy is one of prayer. Her name was Anna, and her whole life was dedicated to praying. This seemingly minor Gospel character was among the first to proclaim that Jesus, the long-awaited Messiah, had come.

What was special about Anna? Her brief story, found in Luke 2:36–38, reveals no startling details. Anna was simply a widow who prayed all the time, both day and night, never leaving the Temple.

What do we make of this? Some of us may feel called to emulate her lifestyle. Most of us probably will not. Our lives are filled with other responsibilities, and we can't spend our whole time praying in a church. But she *just did it. She just prayed.*

Could she have found an excuse not to?

Of course she could have. She was female. Women weren't even allowed into the innermost part of the Temple in Jerusalem.

Men yes, women no.

Anna still prayed.

As an eighty-four-year-old widow (who had been married for only seven years of her life), Anna was one of the more vulnerable members of society. Could she have wallowed in fear and loneliness? Certainly.

But Anna prayed. She prayed and prayed and prayed and prayed some more. Anna longed to see Jesus. Her devotion resounded throughout heaven. Nothing would stop her spiritual hunger.

What about you?

TAKE A STEP AND HE WILL HONOR IT

Just as God honored the prayers of His Son and the prayers of Anna, so He will honor the prayers of men and women who daily live as His disciples. God gave us the privilege to communicate with Him; we have the honor of praying to Him for our own needs and also on behalf of others. Of course, we cannot coerce, manipulate, or force God to answer our desires. We *can* ask Him anything, and then allow Him to answer our prayer in His own timing and will. The prayer of a righteous man or woman is effective, especially when we take the time to align our prayers with God's purposes.

When it comes to some of the items discussed in earlier chapters like committed relationships and your vision from the Word, were you ever discouraged? Does the task before you seem daunting? Be encouraged! It's perfectly okay to not always know where to start. Pray this simple prayer: *"Lord, open doors for me today. Make Your way clear."*

GOD WANTS TO HEAR FROM US TODAY

My favorite verse about prayer is found in 1 Samuel 12:23: "As for me, far be it from me that I should sin against the LORD by failing to pray for you. And I will teach you the way that is good and right." This verse challenges me on a personal level. It tells me that prayer should not be viewed as optional. And, as a personal conviction for myself, I am committed to praying for others regularly.

If you make a similar commitment, as you begin to pray regularly for situations or people, you will see a pattern develop: You trust God, He answers your prayers, and then you see that He is always loving and reliable in His responses. As you become more obedient and faithful in prayer, you will become more aware of God's answers to your requests. Why? Because you have developed a trusting and earnest relationship with your heavenly Father—and He delights in answering your prayers (Psalm 20:4, 37:4). Our personal relationship with God is what makes the difference over time. We are either growing closer to Him through daily prayer or we are moving away from Him. We are each given that choice. Choose wisely!

As you mature in your faith, as your experience of answered prayer grows, you may desire to spend more and more time with the Lord in prayer. Nothing you experience in this world will ever equal the joy of fellowship with your heavenly Father.

Why not begin by talking to your Lord right now? He's waiting.

Applications to Daily Life

1. Have you asked God to teach you how to pray? Do you desire an attitude of prayer?

2. Do you recognize God's answers to your prayers? Do you record these? Or do you take note of them in some other way?

3. Do you pray for others? When you think of someone, try developing the habit of immediately offering that person to God in prayer.

4. Begin praying this prayer every day: "Lord, open doors for me today." Ask God for His daily guidance as you live the disciple's life.

Chapter 7

Opportunities for Action

Therefore,
prepare your minds for action. . . .
1 PETER 1:13

S ince being a daily disciple is a *process,* I believe small events—
I call them *opportunities for action*—can be identified along the
way. As they are recognized and acted upon, these small events
(things that seem to "pop up" in the Christian life) can help men
and women grow from immaturity to maturity in Christ.

As human beings created in the image of God, designed to
become more like His Son, if we pay attention to the opportunities that come our way, the experiences can be priceless. To
give you an idea of what I mean, allow me to share a few examples from my own life.

MY GROWTH AS A DISCIPLE

S omething happened back in 1963 that helped ignite a
hunger in me. Were it not for this action step, the course
of my life could have proceeded quite differently.

When I was working as a high school coach, I met a man
named Don Reeverts. This tall, sharp-looking guy was talking

about something called "Young Life." So I asked him, "What is that?"

He said, "Come and see."

I went to Cherry Creek High School (in Littleton, Colorado) to take in the Young Life experience for myself. It was amazing. More than 250 young people came once a week to hear the gospel, socialize, and be semi-rowdy. *Who says kids can't have fun?* I thought. These young people definitely had fun!

I became convinced that I should begin my own group like this in the high school where I was working. Don encouraged me and helped get me started. I found an older couple that had a huge basement they allowed us to use as a meeting place. Eventually, my group grew to one hundred kids at every meeting.

I experienced great joy as I watched the boys and girls become men and women spiritually. Something about me–the essence of my life's vision–was planted in my heart back then. I began to understand the importance of investing my life in others. Don had planted a seed that would later grow and develop.

A few years later, in 1966, I finally became *convicted* to go back to church regularly. I was now living in Aurora, Colorado, teaching physical education at Hinckley High School in Aurora. My wife and I had decided we might want to start looking for a church. Carolyn had grown up in a Christian home, whereas I had accepted Christ in 1959.

We finally began to attend Galilee Baptist Church. The Christ-centered preaching I heard there began to convict my heart even more. One night, Galilee's pastor came to our home and we told him we wanted to join the church as members. He looked at me and said something startling: "I don't want you to join the church."

You can probably imagine my surprise.

Then, he added, "Do you *know Jesus?*"

I was stunned. In that instant, I realized the truth about how I'd been living. All along, I had been living for myself, rather than for God.

Not long after this, the church held its Easter service. During this service, I made a deeper commitment to God. I went forward during an altar call and was baptized. Immediately afterward, a couple came forward to be assigned to Carolyn and myself. Mr. and Mrs. Jay Oertli became our big brother and big sister.

As my life unfolded further, Jay challenged me to join a Bible study and be discipled. At that point, I recall I gave him my own version of the standard masculine brush-off: "I'm too busy." I claimed to be too immersed in coaching gymnastics and tennis.

Jay never wavered. He and his wife persisted and brought the study into my home. As we began to meet, this sparked the greatest period of Christian growth in my life. The Oertlis were involved in the Navigators ministry, and we went through a two-year, topical discipleship program. Every week that young couple poured their lives into Carolyn and me. Looking back, I realize this was God's way of giving me a wake-up call to committed spiritual growth.

As Christians, we can never assume we will grow simply through osmosis, with no effort on our part. My experiences with Don and Jay led to an even deeper commitment to the disciple's life a few short years later when I met Dan Stavely in 1972 in Boulder.

Dan had been a football coach under Eddie Crowder at the University of Colorado. Everyone called him the "Old Coach." When I walked into Old Coach's office for the first time, the first thing he said to me was very succinct. He took one look at me and said, "Sit down, shorty." I obliged.

Then he asked me if I was in any kind of Christian fellowship. "No, sir."

The Old Coach suggested I begin to attend Fellowship of Christian Athletes (FCA) meetings every week on Mondays at 7 A.M., plus another hour a week with him personally. I took him up on it.

Dan worked with me–and through the process, God worked in my life. The Old Coach used to say to me, "The reason we do discipleship is so you can be a blood-bought, born-again, Satan-hatin', Bible-packin', knee-bendin', Spirit-filled, deep-water-baptized Christian." Truly, the Old Coach understood the importance of building Christlikeness into the younger generation–perhaps better than anyone I have ever met. When I left CU, I joined the ministry of FCA as a result of his influence.

ANOTHER DISCIPLE'S GROWTH

N ancy, the woman I mentioned in an earlier chapter, has her own story to tell. The details are different, but the principles are the same.

I grew up in a Christian home, and I can't point to a specific point of time when I first accepted Christ. He was simply always there, for as long as I can remember. But I can point to times that made a difference in my life as Christ's disciple. The first of these came when I went to college. This was my first real opportunity to meet with other Christians as equals, and these one-on-one relationships made me excited about my faith. But two of my professors were the ones who truly encouraged me to make my faith my own. Up until now, I'd taken my faith as it was handed on to me by my parents, with few questions asked. In high school, I had begun to rebel a little against my parents' authority, and along with that had come some questions in regard to my belief in Christ. But, through the influence of these professors, I began to claim my relationship with Christ as something that was uniquely and personally mine (not my parents'). These two men challenged me to use my intellect hand-in-hand with my faith, so that my mind, too, would become a tool for building the Kingdom of God.

Upon graduation from college, I worked in an inner-city crisis center. There I was confronted with pain and ugliness I had never imagined. An older, more experienced Christian woman took me under her wing. Under her guidance, I learned to pray for each desperate need I confronted. I began to understand that I could not keep my faith to myself. The world desperately needed Christ's Good News.

My marriage was the next turning point in my life. I had always been a very shy person, so insecure that I was afraid to step out and act for fear I would fail. My lack of confidence held me back from being used to the full extent for God's kingdom, but God used my relationship with my husband to finally convince me I was unconditionally loved. This sense of security freed me to reach out to others in new, more confident ways.

Being a mother of young children kept me busy for several years, and during this busy time I turned to God when I was up in the night with a fussy child, while I changed diapers, while I did the laundry—but it was hard to ever find much time to be alone with God. Two years ago, though, my youngest child went to kindergarten. I made a commitment with an older woman to meet once a week to pray and evaluate my life in light of the gospel. Now I am being challenged to go even deeper with Jesus, to put still more of my life in His hands, to let Him use me in new ways.

Looking back at my life, I'm grateful for each person God put along my way—and I'm grateful for their willingness to let God use them.

FIVE KEYS FOR ACTION

M y experience and Nancy's indicate that there are five keys to the process of being a daily disciple. These are points to keep in mind as we disciple others and allow ourselves to be discipled.

❖ *Pursuit* (In my own example, Don, Jay, and Dan all knew they needed to keep pursuing me; I had the sense to not close myself off from their efforts.)

❖ *Commitment* (Without the commitment of others, as well as Nancy's own commitment in response, she wouldn't have gotten anywhere.)

❖ *Openness* (Being receptive to the Holy Spirit's teaching was crucial in both my life and Nancy's.)

❖ *Perseverance* (I didn't always get the message instantly, but Don, Jay, and Dan were *patient and persistent* with me.)

❖ *Lack of selfishness* (When we put ourselves first, we hurt Christ's body here on earth. The manner in which we influence others down the road can be dependent upon simply making one right choice at a certain time—a choice made not just for the sake of ourselves, but for how we will ultimately serve the Kingdom.)

Again, the disciple's life is a *process.* Along the way, though, are small events that by themselves may not seem that significant. But in the scope of the Kingdom they can work together to create a masterpiece, a "finished" product—the mature believer.

Every individual is different. We may not always know which step we take will lead to endeavors that enrich our lives and the lives of those around us to God's glory. But one thing is certain: We'll never know what could have been if we simply allow the opportunities to pass by us.

ON THE ROAD TO EMMAUS

A simple yet profound story comes at the close of the Gospel of Luke. From it I believe we can take away something significant—another example of how we can take advantage of opportunities for action in our lives as daily disciples.

Here is the account of what happened on the road to Emmaus (Luke 24:13–33):

*Now that same day two of them were going to a village called
Emmaus, about seven miles from Jerusalem. They were talking with each other about everything that had happened. As
they talked and discussed these things with each other, Jesus
himself came up and walked along with them; but they were
kept from recognizing him.*

*He asked them, "What are you discussing together as you
walk along?"*

*They stood still, their faces downcast. One of them, named
Cleopas, asked him, "Are you only a visitor to Jerusalem and do
not know the things that have happened there in these days?"*

"What things?" he asked.

*"About Jesus of Nazareth," they replied. "He was a
prophet, powerful in word and deed before God and all the
people. The chief priests and our rulers handed him over to be
sentenced to death, and they crucified him; but we had hoped
that he was the one who was going to redeem Israel. And
what is more, it is the third day since all this took place. In
addition, some of our women amazed us. They went to the
tomb early this morning but didn't find his body. They came
and told us that they had seen a vision of angels, who said he
was alive. Then some of our companions went to the tomb
and found it just as the women had said, but him they did
not see."*

*He said to them, "How foolish you are, and how slow of
heart to believe all that the prophets have spoken! Did not the
Christ have to suffer these things and then enter his glory?"
And beginning with Moses and all the Prophets, he explained
to them what was said in all the Scriptures concerning himself.*

*As they approached the village to which they were going,
Jesus acted as if he were going farther. But they urged him*

strongly, "Stay with us, for it is nearly evening; the day is almost over." So he went in to stay with them.

When he was at the table with them, he took bread, gave thanks, broke it and began to give it to them. Then their eyes were opened and they recognized him, and he disappeared from their sight. They asked each other, "Were not our hearts burning within us while he talked with us on the road and opened the Scriptures to us?"

They got up and returned at once to Jerusalem.

A host of opportunities for action can be gleaned from the story of the road to Emmaus. Consider the following:

❖ *Get into relationships with a few others.* The two disciples on the road to Emmaus were spending time together, even in their confusion and sadness.

❖ *Communicate through prayer and Scripture on spiritual and heart issues.* These two disciples spent time with Jesus discussing the Scriptures, and together with Jesus they came to God in prayer before their meal.

❖ *Allow Jesus to direct your walk; seek and search after the Father's will.* These disciples asked Jesus to accompany them on their journey, and they were clearly open to the insight He gave them.

❖ *When you spend time with other disciples, keep things focused on Christ.* Jesus asked, "What are you discussing together as you walk along?" Their response tells us that they had been talking about Jesus and the events that led to His death.

❖ *Put your trust in God.* These disciples were dismayed by the Crucifixion, but Jesus reminded them to see things from God's perspective rather than a human one.

❖ *Enter into Christ's suffering and brokenness.* These two disciples could think of nothing besides Jesus' death.

❖ *Let Christ open your eyes to His plans—His opportunities for action—for you.* Because these two individuals had been open to what Jesus had to say to them, their eyes were opened and they saw the truth.

❖ *Express to God your willingness to be sent, and embrace His call.* These two people immediately went back to Jerusalem to tell the others the good news. Read Isaiah 6:8–9.

❖ *Open the Scriptures to others.* Luke 24:32 says, "They asked each other, 'Were not our hearts burning within us while he talked with us on the road and opened the Scriptures to us?' " I recommend as a guideline for Bible study no less than once a week for an hour and a half. (If ninety minutes seems like a lot, consider that this is less time than the average person spends *per day* watching television.)

❖ *Ask Christ to stay with you and be your guide.* We don't know the rest of the story, but after their experience with Jesus on the road to Emmaus, I suspect that these two disciples walked with Him daily.

❖ *Understand the message Christ left the disciples; find opportunities to share it.* If we read on past this story a few verses, Luke 24:47 says, " 'And repentance and forgiveness of sins will be preached in his name to all nations, beginning at Jerusalem.' "

❖ *Stay together and struggle together.* Again, we don't know the specific details of these two individuals' lives, but we do know that all the disciples spent time gathering together, sharing their hardships and triumphs.

CHOOSE TODAY

I n the Old Testament we find the story of Abraham, who was a true forerunner of faith. Abraham's life is sprinkled with opportunities for action. Time after time, Abraham made a choice to seek God first (Matthew 6:33). The life of Abraham is an Old Testament parallel for the New Testament believer's life.

Bit by bit, little by little, as we invest more, we will experience a deepening of spiritual maturity. One small step may be all we need to get us moving in the right direction today. Whenever we move in the direction God wants, at each point–each step–we can find an expanded vision of His purposes, an increase in our own confidence, and a heightened zeal and joy in our life.

I could have easily told Don Reeverts that the young bouncy

crowd just wasn't for me. I could have blown Jay Oertli off. There were times when the hour Dan Stavely had reserved for me could have simply gone unattended.

We all have our excuses in life—those old standbys we know few people will challenge, much less overcome. We use these excuses to avoid opportunities that may lead somewhere substantial in the Kingdom.

What about you? If someone asked you to write a chapter about the steps of your own life, how would it read? Can you look back and see God at work? When you do look back, can you admit you still have a long way to go?

Think about it.

Once again, no one else can write your story for you. You determine the paths you will take. When an opportunity arises to move forward, there *is* something you can do. *Move!*

Henry Blackaby, the author of *Experiencing God,* spoke in my area not long ago, and I had the chance to hear him. This is one of the principles he mentioned: *There is never a coincidence in the life of a Christian.*

Chew on that one for a moment. Things that happen to us, some of which may seem entirely "by accident," just might very well be smack dab in the middle of God's purposes for our lives.

So, this leads to an important question. . . .

What non-coincidence is staring down *at you* right now? Anything come to mind? If nothing of note seems to have happened yet, trust me, friend, something is going to unfold.

Opportunities for growth in your life as a daily disciple *will* occur. Don't miss them.

APPLICATIONS TO DAILY LIFE

Consider the five keys we mentioned in this chapter in the light of your own life:

1. Are you pursuing relationships? Is another disciple pursuing you?

2. Are these committed relationships?

3. Are you open to the Holy Spirit's teaching?

4. Do you persevere in your relationships? Or do you tend to give up easily?

5. Are you willing to put others first, before yourself?

CHAPTER 8

Reconciliation

All this is from God,
who reconciled us to himself through Christ
and gave us the ministry of reconciliation.
2 CORINTHIANS 5:18

S omeone asked me this question recently: What does reconciliation have to do with a disciple's daily life?

Reconciliation has everything to do with being a disciple. In a spiritual sense, reconciliation means that God has not counted our sins against us, but has forgiven us through Christ. In an interpersonal sense, reconciliation means if we have anything against our brother or sister, we are to "leave the altar" (Matthew 5:23–24) and go be reconciled to our brother or sister. In a denominational sense, we are to live in unity with the body of believers, maintaining a commitment to our unique qualities—as long as they align with God's Word. Meanwhile, we must be quick to listen, slow to speak, and slow to anger about another person's beliefs.

Through reconciliation, we *become* representatives or ambassadors of Christ, so God can reach others with the gospel through us. If we are not first reconciled to our heavenly Father, we cannot live the disciple's life.

How, then, do we develop or attain a reconciling spirit? We don't. But as we yield ourselves to the Lord Jesus Christ, He can make a positive difference in others through us. It's not about our efforts; it's about God working through our lives. As 2 Corinthians 5:17–21 teaches, "Therefore, if anyone is in Christ, he is a new creation; the old has gone, the new has come! All this is from God, who reconciled us to himself through Christ and gave us the ministry of reconciliation: that God was reconciling the world to himself in Christ, not counting men's sins against them. And he has committed to us the message of reconciliation. We are therefore Christ's ambassadors, as though God were making his appeal through us. We implore you on Christ's behalf: Be reconciled to God. God made him who had no sin to be sin for us, so that in him we might become the righteousness of God."

This issue of reconciliation cuts to the heart of where we are. Are we really serious about living as disciples of Jesus Christ?

OKLAHOMA CITY— RECONCILIATION IN THE AFTERMATH OF THE BOMBING

One of the powerful forces that can keep us from becoming reconcilers is our hidden prejudices. The following story shows how these can make us very inadequate at reconciliation, for they keep us from understanding people's pain.

I was in Oklahoma City in April of 1995, about a week after the bombing of the Alfred P. Murrah Federal Building where 169 people lost their lives through an act of hatred and terrorism. Alvin Simpkins (who was then the Central Regional Director for Promise Keepers) and I went into the city to speak with pastors

Daily DISCIPLES

about their terrible losses caused by the bombing. Alvin insisted that we also go and view the site of the destruction.

We traveled downtown, and I could not believe the devastation, the broken glass strewn for miles, the myriad police, firemen, rescue vehicles, recovery personnel, and volunteer workers. We couldn't get closer than three blocks from the actual building, because the authorities had put up chain-link fences around the perimeter of the blast site. I stood at the fence, solemnly looking at what was left of the building. Then, behind me, I heard something out of the ordinary.

God was at work, through Alvin, who was witnessing to a drunken man who had been rummaging through a nearby trash bin for aluminum cans so he could sell them to get cash for another drink. Alvin was telling this repulsive guy about Jesus Christ and His love. I was taken aback. As Alvin came over to me and introduced this pitiful individual to me, I actually thought (and later said), *How can you witness to this guy—he's repulsive!* Now, like Paul Harvey would say. . .the *rest* of the story.

Alvin told me that it was easy for him to share Jesus with the man because he had watched his father, a Baptist pastor, rummage through dumpsters to collect aluminum cans to cash in for money to feed Alvin's family. His father always witnessed to everyone about Christ's love, even as he was rummaging through the trash. The story Alvin related was incredible.

God's convicting spirit came upon me so strongly I began to weep. I was overwhelmed with total humiliation for my own lack of concern for my brother's pain and suffering. Personally, I had been blessed with so much—and then I had failed to relate to how little my brothers around me might have. I confessed to Alvin my lack of sensitivity. Since that day, I have made an intentional decision to love my less fortunate brothers and sisters.

Now when I look at my brothers and sisters, I feel God's love convict me to never again "pass by" or ignore the person God has created. God's work of grace in my life concerning my personal prejudice serves as a reminder for me of how He can forgive anyone who has harbored anything from hate to indifference toward others. Through this experience, God has helped me to truly understand how to love my neighbor as myself. I have learned never to judge someone else. Hopefully, through my being sincere and transparent, others can sense my love for them.

To Build Up, Not Tear Down

Judging people is a major sin that keeps us from being reconcilers. Yet we have a Savior and Lord Who didn't condemn people who were different from Him; in fact, He actually hung out with them. We are called to *build up* the body of Christ, not tear it down with criticisms or unrealistic expectations. A daily disciple of Christ needs to understand this.

In his book *Building Up One Another*, Gene Getz, drawing from Jesus' prayer in John 17:20–23, gives a graphic portrayal of the members of the body of Christ. He discusses three core truths:

1. Interdependence: No individual can function effectively in isolation and alone.

2. Humility: No member of Christ's body should feel more important than any other member of Christ's body.

3. Unity: Every Christian should work hard at creating
    unity in the body of Christ.[1]

The "body metaphor" illustrates that Christians (whether
we like it or not) are members of one another. That's why we
need to take seriously what the Bible says about loving one
another.

The Apostle Paul uses the body metaphor in 1 Corinthians
to get our attention. He says, "Now the body is not made up of
one part but of many. . . . God has arranged the parts in the
body, every one of them, just as he wanted them to be. If they
were all one part, where would the body be? As it is, there are
many parts, but one body. . . . There should be no division in
the body, but that its parts should have equal concern for each
other" (12:14, 18–20, 25). Paul, clearly, is trying to get us to
understand that we really do need each other. We are not independent but dependent. What a powerful witness to a watching
world when the body comes together to act the way a body can
and should!

A woman I'll call Salli tells this story about "body unity":

*I've known Shirley for years. Our kids have gone to the same
school, we've lived in the same neighborhood, we've attended
the same church. We've even led the same Bible study groups
now and then. But I never liked her.*

*For one thing, Shirley was one of those perfect people. Her
house was always spotlessly clean, no matter when you
stopped by, and her hair was always just so, and she'd never
gained a pound since she was eighteen. I always felt like a
slightly chubby slob next to her.*

But that wouldn't have been so bad if Shirley hadn't

always had to be right. No matter what topic came up, she always knew more than anyone else. No matter what group she was in, the rest of us always had to do things her way. She drove me crazy.

And then one Sunday, our pastor preached about forgiveness. I'd heard sermons like that a hundred times before and never batted an eye. I was certain I didn't harbor any unforgiveness in my heart; after all, I thought, I don't have any enemies. But that particular Sunday as I sat there listening, my gaze happened to fall on Shirley. I felt as though the Holy Spirit was speaking directly to me, nudging me to examine my own heart.

I began to pray that God would give me love for Shirley. And then I prayed that He would help me to understand her better. To my amazement, I began to see she wasn't as self-assured and arrogant as I had always thought. Just like me, she was insecure sometimes. I realized she came on so strong because she was trying to compensate for her own worries. And when I reached out to her as a real friend, she immediately reached right back to me.

Shirley and I still don't always get along. But I can truly say I love her. More than that, I know I need her. After all, we're both members of Christ's body. If I said I didn't need Shirley, that would be about as silly as if my toe tried to say it didn't need my eye.

As Salli learned, we cannot overlook any member of Christ's body. If we are to function effectively in the world, we need to each experience unity with all the others.

THE CASE OF THE STOLEN VAN

A nother area where reconciliation is needed is between different types of churches. Consider the story of two very different churches in the Denver area; through circumstances that even a secular newspaper referred to as "divine intervention," somehow they came together.

Quinn Wilhelm, a theft investigations detective for the police department in Lakewood, Colorado (a Denver suburb), was assigned to the case of a stolen 1986 Dodge minivan. The individual from whom the van was stolen was the chairman of the deacon board at Mount Carmel Missionary Baptist Church. Despite the strain of the circumstances that introduced them to one another, Wilhelm and the board chairman enjoyed each other's company. Wilhelm received an invitation to a Mount Carmel service.

Eventually, he responded to that invitation. Upon attending the service at Mount Carmel, Wilhelm learned that the church was having difficulty meeting their upcoming payment of $30,000 for their new building. Wilhelm brought the issue to the attention of his own church, Christ Episcopal, and within a few days they had raised over $30,000. Wilhelm returned to Mount Carmel and informed them of the bad news and the good news: He hadn't recovered the van, but he did have a check for them that was going to help make their payment. According to Mount Carmel's minister, after Wilhelm's presentation to the church, "there was a moment of silence, and then the congregation erupted in praise and joy."

The story doesn't end here. As Wilhelm put it, "This whole thing is not just about money. It's about relationships." Since that time, Christ Episcopal, a mostly white church, and Mount Carmel, a predominantly black church, have been involved in a host of ongoing activities with one another. These have included joint worship services and other get-togethers. Mount Carmel's pastor has preached at Christ Episcopal's services; likewise, Mount Carmel has had Christ Episcopal's rector come and speak at their services. The two churches have become more and more acclimated to each other's worship style. Wilhelm commented, "Episcopalians are fairly conservative and formal. The Mount Carmel congregation is more outgoing, more informal. I'd never worked up a sweat at church before."

Two churches. Different denominations. Different ethnic makeup. A stolen van. . .

Who would have thought?

Clearly, there are no limits to what the Lord can do among His followers if we will be obedient.

The secular newspaper the *Denver Post* (not normally known as a source of favorable opinions toward things Christ-centered) actually ran an editorial commentary shortly after the story was first reported about the two churches. The column noted, in part:

> *The* Denver Post *reported last week that predominantly black Mount Carmel Community [sic] Baptist Church and mostly white Christ Episcopal Church have formed a kind of partnership in which services will be held jointly at least three times a year.*
>
> *The cooperative arrangement unexpectedly grew out of an incident involving a stolen van, an occurrence that provoked members of Christ Episcopal to contribute over $30,000 to the Mount Carmel building fund.*
>
> *As the Rev. Harold Hicks of Mount Carmel put it, "The*

great thing is that this has fostered relationships across racial and denominational lines. This is a major blessing."

Few would disagree, but what is not so well known is that similar events have been happening in many American communities.

In St. Louis, two major church groups, after long years of going separate ways, have jointly sponsored a program featuring joint worship services and other steps aimed at racial reconciliation. In Cincinnati, two churches, one Catholic, the other Baptist, have formed a prayer partnership.

In Chicago, the mostly white Hope Presbyterian and the mostly black Hope Church have shared meals, retreats, and worship services for the last seven years. There are similar reports coming out of Dayton and Chattanooga and a number of other U.S. cities. . . .

There is, of course, a long way to go before Sunday morning looks like the rest of the week, but given the long period in which there had been little change in worship patterns, the news recently has been uniformly encouraging.[2]

The ministry work and relationship between the two churches carries on today.

WHY RECONCILIATION IS A MAIN ASPECT OF LIVING THE DISCIPLE'S LIFE

As Jesus told us through His prayer to God the Father in John 17:23, when we as His followers are " 'brought to complete unity,' " the world *will* take notice. Through us, the world can *know*, as Jesus said in prayer, " 'that you sent me and have loved them even as you have loved me.' " As one part of the body of Christ, we must recognize the entire body, acknowledging that God created all of us uniquely with a specific function that can benefit the entire body.

What does this mean practically? God wants us to open up in areas we've never been open to before. This frequently requires attitude adjustments for us. We need a reconciling, servant-oriented spirit in our dealings with others. This isn't always easy; sometimes it's even painful. And yet any adjustments God expects us to make in our lives and hearts are for our own good. Ultimately, of course, these adjustments also lead to the greater good of the Good News, the message of Christ.

When we allow God to use us to act as reconcilers, we show His love to others. We can't be daily disciples if we don't.

Will we act as one body?

The outside world is watching.

APPLICATIONS TO DAILY LIFE

1. Is there someone you have judged? Have you taken steps to reconcile with this individual?

2. How can your local church participate in reconciliation? What practical ways as a body can you show God's love to others?

CHAPTER 9

Passing on the Mantle

We will tell the next generation
the praiseworthy deeds of the LORD,
his power, and the wonders he has done.
He decreed statutes for Jacob
and established the law in Israel,
which he commanded our forefathers
to teach their children,
so the next generation would know them,
even the children yet to be born,
and they in turn would tell their children.
Then they would put their trust in God
and would not forget his deeds
but would keep his commands.
PSALM 78:4–7

I f the truth be told, disciplehood as a way of life is never more than one generation away from extinction.

That's a disturbing notion. So far in this book we've been thinking about being a disciple from the adult perspective. All too often we overlook the fact that in a very real sense parents have the opportunity to disciple their children in Christ.

When we think of "passing on the mantle," we may visualize a garment or piece of jewelry or something else we literally pass on to our heirs: something tangible. Or the old adage of "filling our parents' shoes" may come to mind. When we speak

in spiritual terms, however, passing on the mantle means something a little different; it means we train and nurture our children in the Lord.

Training a child in the spiritual sense means we are positive
role models; we provide them with attainable goals and guidelines; and most of all, we "go the distance"—in other words, we
see "the project" through to completion. We can't do any of
this, though, if first and foremost we lack a personal experience
of spiritual growth. Along with that, we must put into practice
a drastic reduction in our self-focused behavior.

From the time a child is born, one way or another, as parents we are engaged in the process of "passing it on." Probably
the majority of us don't formulate a concept of spiritual heritage for our children immediately after they are born. We may
be too overwhelmed with the myriad practical details that go
along with adding a child to our lives.

But if we hope to pass on a spiritual mantle to our children,
we must put effort into it. We need to think carefully *what* we
hope to communicate spiritually to our children and *how* we want
to do it. Here are my recommendations.

As Christian mothers or fathers, we must establish a family
habit of prayer, a time when we thank the Lord together for His
goodness and mercy. We also need to establish a Bible reading
time (and possibly a time for singing together as well). Beginning at birth, we parents need to pray over our children, peti-
tioning the Lord for their health, their spiritual growth, and
their future. As children begin to walk and talk, meal times are
good opportunities to thank the Lord for what He has provided.
As children grow still older, they should be encouraged to join
in family prayer—a special time of prayer for family needs.

A son I know has these memories of family devotions:

I remember very vividly when I was a young boy—starting as early as the age of six and well into my teen years—the Bible study time at our house. Every night, my brother, myself, and my mom and dad would take time after dinner as a family. We took only about half an hour usually; it wasn't very long and drawn out. (I guess it seemed longer when I was a kid.) But the neatest thing I remember is that we read Scripture together. We read a Bible passage and even had a book called Little Visits with God *that sort of kept my brother and me entertained when we were real young. We worked on Scripture memorization, which I remember finding enjoyable and chal- lenging. I recall one of the verses particularly, the one about the wise and foolish builders, found in Matthew. It talks about the man who built his house upon the rock and also the man who built his house upon the sand. I can honestly say I took that to heart as I grew older. I always remembered those verses. In hard times the verses I learned during our family Bible study stayed embedded in my heart.*

There is no single *right* way to do family devotions; what works for one family may not work for another—and vice versa. One family I know takes time each week to share "God's sur- prises" in their lives. This encourages children to develop the habit of thanking God for all His many and varied blessings. Another family has a brief time of prayer each morning before family members all head off in their various directions. Whatever works for your family's personalities and schedules, the important thing is that you make a habit of including God in your family life.

I also think a parent needs to pray a daily bedtime prayer over each child from the time he or she is born until adolescence.

At that point, by mutual consent, you may want to cease this activity (but if the child requests that the bedtime prayer continue after that point, what a wonderful bonus). Either way, I encourage parents to continue in fervent prayer for their children—*and* assure sons and daughters verbally that parental love, support, and prayer will continue for the rest of their lives. At that same time, while older children may not feel comfortable praying out loud, we can encourage them to develop their own individual prayer time. As this son's testimony indicates, perhaps the best way to do this is to make sure our children are aware that we pray.

> *My dad instilled the value of prayer in me by doing it himself.*
> *I would watch him pray, as we would in our Bible study,*
> *and this proved to be a big part of the discipleship process for*
> *me. A few times when I was in college and was struggling, he*
> *would always let me know he was praying for me. He would*
> *always remind me that there's a spiritual side to life. Whether*
> *I wanted to hear it at the time or not, I understood that*
> *through the power of prayer, God would and could get ahold of*
> *our hearts—get ahold of my heart and change my attitude.*

We still carry on our habit of prayer today when I visit with him and we go hunting or fishing. When we spend time in the car, we use the "down" time we have together praying and talking about what's going on in our lives.

PASSING ON THE BLESSING

Within certain Jewish traditions, at age thirteen young men have a "bar mitzvah" and young women go through a "bat mitzvah" to recognize their arrival into adulthood. This event brings a sense of "completion" and positive self-esteem to the individual being recognized. Once the teenage years are reached, I think children benefit from this sort of ceremonial moment when parents, friends, and church family give them a "blessing"–a special, specific acknowledgment of all that we want God to bestow on them. In many cultures a "rite of passage" type of ceremony is performed to acknowledge that a boy or girl has passed into manhood or womanhood. Unfortunately, as Christians we have few, if any, ceremonies that reinforce the importance of "the blessing." I believe that such events can act as a critical affirmation of the passage to adulthood for the next generation.

In the Bible's first book, Genesis, three chapters (27, 48, and 49) tell of parents giving and children receiving the blessing. These passages describe how Isaac blessed Jacob, and then how Israel (Jacob) blessed his sons (who represented the twelve historic tribes). Genesis 27:25–29 describes the blessing this way:

Then he said, "My son, bring me some of your game to eat, so that I may give you my blessing."

Jacob brought it to him and he ate; and he brought some wine and he drank. Then his father Isaac said to him, "Come here, my son, and kiss me."

So he went to him and kissed him. When Isaac caught the smell of his clothes, he blessed him and said, "Ah, the smell of my son is like the smell of a field that the LORD has blessed. May God give you of heaven's dew and of earth's richness—an abundance of grain and new wine. May nations serve you and peoples bow down to you. Be lord over your brothers, and may the sons of your mother bow down to you. May those who curse you be cursed and those who bless you be blessed."

One interesting note about this passage is that Jacob received the blessing that was intended to go to his brother, Esau. In Old Testament times, apparently once the blessing was given, it was irrevocable. Esau, like many in our modern day who are "floundering" around in search of something (an identity?), was sent into quite a tailspin as a result of missing out on this blessing from his father.

In their book titled *The Blessing,* authors Gary Smalley and John Trent share how to give a son or daughter a personal blessing. The five components of the biblical blessing (derived from the Genesis 27 passage), according to Smalley and Trent, are:

1. meaningful touch;

2. a spoken message;

3. attaching high value to the individual;

4. picturing a special future for the child; and

5. an active commitment to that young person.[1]

(Interestingly, the paperback version of *The Blessing* is carried by a secular publisher, and it has remained in print for many years—evidence, perhaps, that even those who are not committed Christians still yearn for the affirmation that comes with the blessing?)

As Christian parents, I recommend we release our sons and daughters into manhood and womanhood by giving them "the blessing," whether we do this as a private moment between individuals or as a formal ceremony. Many Christian men and women have never received this blessing, and consequently they may not feel any conscious awareness of their passage into spiritual adulthood. Those who never experience this release will not know it as a model to pass on to their own children, so those of us who *are* familiar with this concept need to actively model it for the rest of Christ's body (yet another way we can help each other walk as daily disciples).

A daughter named Rachel shares this experience of being blessed by her mother:

I'm a young woman now. I'm not a little kid any more, and last year my mom did this really neat thing that helped me feel more excited about growing up. It wasn't a big deal, because I had told her I'd be embarrassed if there were other people there, so just she and I went to our church one evening when no one else was there. We went up to the front, and my mom put her hands on my shoulders and prayed for me. She thanked God for creating me, and she asked God to go with me as I walked out into womanhood. She went on to thank God for all the special gifts He had given me, and she asked Him to show me how to use those gifts now that I was no longer a child. And then she and I talked a long time. She told me all the things she liked about me, all the ways she had seen God using me, and we talked about the future and

145

some of my dreams. And then she told me how much she loved me and promised that she would always be there for me, even when I move out on my own. We both cried a little. Since then, I haven't felt as confused about who I am as I used to. I feel closer to God, too. I've started thinking about a lot of things, and I keep taking them to God, asking for His wisdom. I know He's leading me into the life He wants for me. It's really exciting.

A young man named Eric shares a different experience of being blessed by his father:

As a son, the most memorable statement I've heard from my father—and he says this to other people when I'm around— "Eric is not only my son, he is also my brother in Christ." This statement is an example of my father releasing me to be my own person. That says to me that I am responsible spiritually for my own actions, and it also says to me that he is just as accountable to me as I have been to him in my growing up years. Not only am I his earthly son, but spiritually I am his brother in Christ. My father has given me the right as a man to pray for him, watch out for him, even rebuke him. This is a humbling act that changes the parent-child relationship. It allows us to go to the Word of God together, as equals.

Since our culture has no tradition that provides us with a formula for blessing our children, we need to develop our own. Again, what works for one family may not work for everyone else. We may want a private "ceremony" as Rachel and her mother did—or our "blessing" may simply be an understanding between our children and us, as with Eric and his dad. But either way, our children need to be clear that this blessing is a real factor in their lives.

Here is my advice to each of you, no matter how old you may be: If you have not received or given the biblical blessing, seek it out from your parents and give it to your children. Obviously, in some cases parents may be deceased or otherwise not available. If that's the case, find a "mentor" to give you the blessing. You may be pleasantly surprised at how this can bring peace and completion to your life. If you are a pastor reading this, you might consider including the blessing ceremony as part of your services; it can be an indispensable element of positive church "body life."

FINDING TIME

If I could offer parents one other word of advice, it would be this: Make sure you schedule time, individual time, with each of your sons or daughters to do some activity they enjoy doing. This is an important part of "passing on the mantle," beginning with the early formative years (ages one to seven). A consistent habit of enjoying each child's activity choice—ideally on a weekly basis—is critical to a parent's ability to communicate spiritually with that child. Spending time together like this conveys to the child his or her uniqueness and value. And children who know their parents value and love them can more easily understand that the Lord loves and values them even more.

Invest yourself in your child's life. As children continue to grow, an established pattern of "favorite thing time" helps ensure that children and parents have regular one-on-one time together–and this gives them a platform, also, on which to build spiritual matters. Typically, children who have received this regular one-on-one time with their parents will be more open down the road to a still deeper discipling process, rather than being rebellious and rejecting.

I know many parents who might say that setting aside regular time like this is impossible, what with their jobs and their time schedule. I encourage you to make your children a priority. Children grow all too quickly. In all likelihood, your professional career will be years longer than the years you spend in active parenting. Don't miss out on these critical years.

Once a child is born, parenting is no longer an activity that can wait until it's more convenient. If children are rejected or ignored during the years they spend living in their parents' household, we are much more likely to lose them in later years . . .and possibly for life. The child that is not loved and discipled at a young age may grow up to be rebellious; if parents do not train their children for the Lord, then eventually they will be trained instead by a secular society.

THE WORD AS A GUIDE

The Bible reveals a great deal about passing on the legacy of Christ to the next generation. A few prime examples emerge in 2 Timothy: "And the things you have heard me say in the presence of many witnesses entrust to reliable men who will also be qualified to teach others" (2:2). A few verses later comes this challenge: "Do your best to present yourself to God as one approved, a workman who does not need to be ashamed and who correctly handles the word of truth" (2:15). The younger generation of disciples can then take hold of this charge (2:22–24): "Flee the evil desires of youth, and pursue righteousness, faith, love and peace, along with those who call on the Lord out of a pure heart. Don't have anything to do with foolish and stupid arguments, because you know they produce quarrels. And the Lord's servant must not quarrel; instead, he must be kind to everyone, *able to teach*, not resentful" (emphasis added).

Timothy was on the receiving end of many discipleship directives from Paul. In turn, I am sure Timothy passed on the teaching he received to a younger protégé–a heritage of discipling that continued on and on and on. We can create a similar chain of daily disciples that extends through our children's lives and on into the lives of their children. Some parents may not know how to get started; they may not understand how to move beyond merely raising children to discipling them. If so, here's yet another example of the benefit we can gain from talking with a trusted friend, someone who would be a good person from whom to glean these skills.

Jewish tradition, based on the Torah, places a strong emphasis on passing the spiritual heritage down from one generation to the next. Beginning early in the Old Testament, the instruction is firm: "These commandments that I give you today are to be upon your hearts. Impress them on your children. Talk about them when you sit at home and when you walk along the road, when you lie down and when you get up. Tie them as symbols on your hands and bind them on your foreheads. Write them on the doorframes of your houses and on your gates" (Deuteronomy 6:6–9). From the very beginning, Yahweh has made clear how much He wants us to "pass on the mantle."

But we can't force this mantle onto our children. The goal should always be that the next generation *absorbs* Scripture, rather than has it force-fed to them. When Scripture is presented in a relevant way that relates to a child's life, this can make all the difference. Children need to see what Scripture means in their parents' lives; that's why parents should never act bored or lifeless when they share Scripture. Do we adults find God's Word exciting? When we do, the Scripture that means the most to us is a great place to start as we share with our children.

Also, parents shouldn't worry that children aren't old enough to understand the true depths and nuances of biblical meaning; young people will absorb whatever they are ready to hear. As parents, let's trust the Holy Spirit to open our children's ears. After all, God has promised that His Word will not return to Him empty, but will accomplish that which He desires (Isaiah 55:11). Sharing Scripture with our children is worth the investment of some of our time and innovation.

A GENERATION AT RISK

M uch has been written and said about the members of the next generation. I just returned from a conference where one of the speakers stated that according to one study, approximately 80 percent of young men and women *who grew up in the church* no longer attend regular services. Not only are we apparently failing miserably at reaching those outside the body of Christ, we are failing to disciple those who are right in our midst.

At the beginning of the chapter, we made the point that daily discipleship as a way of life is never more than one generation away from going the way of the dinosaur. The future depends on those of us in the older generation and how we choose to relate to our sons and daughters. Steve Farrar puts the challenge in these succinct terms:

"You cannot impart that which you do not possess. I can't expect something out of my kids that does not exist in my own heart; character isn't something you mandate, it's something you model. And if you are spending your life chasing after external accomplishments rather than internal character, it will show. Count on it, friend, eventually it will show."[2]

Our road may be long and hard, but along the disciple's daily journey, the well–God–never runs dry. In Christ, we have living water. Let's make sure we pass that water along to the thirsty generations to come.

Probably the best way to pass on the mantle of faith to our children is to make certain that our own faith is a living, healthy reality in our lives. Listen to the words of this child as he talks about his parents:

Many times I've seen my parents go through pretty fiery trials, maybe financially or when they've lost a loved one, and the way they've handled that–through trusting in God, through praying to God, through referring to Scripture, through memorizing Scripture–has taught me well. I've never had any sense that they've turned away from God, no matter what happens. In fact, it's always been the opposite: They've drawn closer to God. I've learned a lot from their example.

YOUR HERITAGE

We all have a heritage to pass along, even if we're not parents. Those of us who are childless still have opportunities to make a difference in a young person's life, as this young woman's experience demonstrates:

> *Lydia is one of my mother's closest friends, but she's my friend, too. Ever since I was little, I loved whenever she came over, because she always talked to me like I was someone she was really interested in, like I wasn't just a little kid to her. Now that I'm a teenager, I'm really glad she's my friend. There's lots of stuff in my life that I'd be uncomfortable talking over with my mother, but I can always go to Lydia with a problem. She does a lot of work for overseas missions, and she's gotten me excited about helping out with some projects. I really like the feeling that I can make a difference in the world. I know she prays for me everyday, and I know I can always count on her. I want to get to know God the way she does so that one day I can help other kids the way she's helped me.*

You may not think you have any opportunity to pass on your heritage of faith to the younger generation—but look around you. There may be a young person with whom you have contact who needs your love and influence.

APPLICATIONS TO DAILY LIFE

1. If you are a parent, think through and then write out the ways you are discipling your child. Or, if you happen to be just getting started as a parent, spell out how you plan to disciple your child. Consider also asking your children (if they are old enough to understand) to write out their thoughts about how you have discipled them and how they've felt through the process. If you are not a parent, make a list of the young people with whom you have contact. List some ways you could begin discipling them.

2. Write your personal story of how your parents (or another adult) discipled you. If your parents are still living, consider sending this "story" to them as an expression of your gratitude.

CHAPTER 10

Multiplication and Small Groups

And the word of God increased;
and the number of the disciples multiplied. . .greatly. . . .
ACTS 6:7 KJV

And let us consider how we may
spur one another on toward love and good deeds.
Let us not give up meeting together,
as some are in the habit of doing,
but let us encourage one another—
and all the more as you see the Day approaching.
HEBREWS 10:24–25

W e've already discussed the importance of relationships
in the life of the daily disciple. The gospel of Christ is
one of love—and how can we demonstrate our love if we are not
in close, committed relationships with others? Small groups are
one opportunity we have to form and build a network of love
and commitment between the members of Christ's body.

That's why small groups are also such a powerful way to
spread the Good News of Jesus. An important question I think
the Church needs to ask is whether or not we are going to be a
movement of God or merely a monument of God. Do we want
to be something alive and growing—or do we want to be as solid

and motionless as rock? Multiplication and small groups are ways to really get moving.

In the world of mathematics, we are all familiar with the four commonly understood ways to calculate one number with another: addition, subtraction, multiplication, and division. Subtracting and dividing the number of disciples in the body of Christ would, naturally, not be good goals. This leaves two obvious choices.

Although most churches would probably state that they would like to *add* members to their congregations, in reality the most prolific plan of action is to *multiply* them. This brings us to the principle of multiplication as it relates to the disciple's life. When we reach out to more than one person at a time, we can multiply Christ's disciples.

THE EARLY CHURCH

I f you want to see an example of how this principle of multiplying disciples works out in action, take a look at the account in Acts. Early on in Acts we get a picture of the growth in the young church and the importance of the fellowship and relationship of the believers. After Pentecost, and the filling of the Holy Spirit, the Christians began to meet:

They devoted themselves to the apostles' teaching and to the fellowship, to the breaking of bread and to prayer. Everyone was filled with awe, and many wonders and miraculous signs were done by the apostles. All the believers were together and had everything in common. Selling their possessions and

*goods, they gave to anyone as he had need. Every day they
continued to meet together in the temple courts. They broke
bread in their homes and ate together with glad and sincere
hearts, praising God and enjoying the favor of all the people.
And the Lord* added to their number daily *those who were
being saved.* ACTS 2:42–47, emphasis added

It is sad–yet evident–how far removed the modern-day
Church resides from this account. As Acts picks up the story of
Christianity after the record of Christ found in the four Gos-
pels, try to imagine how the account might read if somebody
attempted to write an "Acts" about the current state of the
Church in America. We may find reality a bit discouraging–but
Acts challenges us to "lifestyle discipleship" that should be car-
ried on until the return of Christ.

THE INFORMAL LIFE OF
THE DAILY DISCIPLE

Sometimes when we see that reality falls so short of the
ideal, we simply give up and don't rise to the challenge.
We may feel too overwhelmed to even make a start. When it
comes to the principle of multiplication as it relates to the disciple's life, I'd like to suggest that one thing everybody can do
is back up a few steps to something less "formal" or structured.
Preferably, we won't take up permanent residence here, but it's
a good place to start.

Most of us had someone we can think of in our lives about

whom we could say, "Yes, he or she influenced me for the better"—even if this person's influence wasn't specifically spiritual. When it comes to the principle of multiplication, we will see no multiplying if we do not influence other people's lives. All of us can probably remember some of the key things about the people who influenced us that made them effective. In the same way, I believe we can model some very simple, practical things that will help us gain the kind of positive influence that will lead to multiplying within Christ's body. I've outlined some of these practical principles in the following list:

❖ *Faithfulness.* Be reliable, someone who can be counted on at all times.

❖ *The ability to listen.* Make sure others "have your ear" when they need it. Take things in rather than speak frequently.

❖ *Integrity.* Be straightforward. Don't allow impure motives to taint your actions.

❖ *Naturalness.* Demonstrate transparency and sincerity.

❖ *Understanding.* Be willing to give the benefit of the doubt. Look for ways to understand rather than criticize.

❖ *Eternity-focused.* Relate to others, remembering always that souls matter more than anything.

❖ *Trustworthiness of speech.* Make sure your yes means yes

and your no means no. When you say you are going to do something, the listener can take your word to the bank. Keep your promises.

❖ *Encouragement.* Communicate positively rather than focusing on the negative; be on the lookout for ways to express appreciation toward others. "Major" in praising people.

These eight characteristics of interaction will go a long way toward multiplying your sphere of influence.

I'm not talking here about quitting your job, or selling all of your possessions so that you can go out and spend your life discipling numerous people full-time. Some persons may be called to that, but most are not. Most of us, however, are already in numerous relationships (with varying levels of commitment). When we utilize the above eight characteristics of interaction, we can take these already existing relationships into the realm of discipleship. As we have direct influences for Christ in people's lives in any number of ways, we will help the body of Christ to "multiply." This form of discipling doesn't necessarily involve a career choice so much as it does a lifestyle, a way of interacting. Through our relationships, we help people follow Christ in different aspects of their lives. You may be helping one person with her prayer life, and another with his financial problems, and yet another with her marital struggles. . .and so on.

WHERE SMALL GROUPS FIT

T here are two trends occurring today. One is a continued erosion in the number of committed men and women who fervently seek Christlikeness for their lives in the context of the local church. The other, seemingly contradictory, trend is an increased interest in small groups within the church. (According to recent statistics, the number of small groups and cell groups in the church has more than doubled in the past eight years.[1]) While the increased interest in small group fellowship points (possibly) to an encouraging future, clearly there is much work to be done.

My interest in small groups has heightened over the course of the last several years. As ministries like Promise Keepers continue to challenge men to be involved in small groups, similar ministries for women have emerged, such as Women of Faith, Heritage Keepers, Aspiring Women, and others. Clearly, small group discussion isn't going to die out.

When we Christians come back from one of these ministry conferences (or something else in our lives that is similarly convicting), probably the very least we can do is ask, "Who can I share with?" Or perhaps we will pray, "Lord, direct me to someone I can share with." Many of us, as we start, don't know what we should do, but God will honor that first step of surrender to His direction.

Small group ministry evokes tremendous excitement on my part because it is an area in which I've seen changes for the better in Christians. Various things in the Christian life may ignite us, but what causes lasting change is day-to-day growth and investment. Walking the disciple's daily path is far easier when we have close companions along the way; in fact, as we've already said, we *can't* truly be Christ's disciples if we isolate ourselves from loving, committed relationships with others. Small groups may not be the only way to form these relationships, but they are a very fruitful one. I liken it to the ripple effect of dropping a stone in a pool of water; in a small group, as the Spirit works in one person's life, His influence spreads from person to person in an ever-widening circle of blessing.

WHY A SMALL GROUP?

Throughout the history of the Church, small groups have been important. Earlier in this chapter we took a closer look at the first Christians in the Book of Acts, and clearly those young pioneers of the Christian faith took part in what today might be considered small group fellowship—"They devoted themselves to the apostles' teaching and to the fellowship, to the breaking of bread and to prayer" (Acts 2:42). As the decades and centuries have passed in the Church, those in the body of Christ have frequently flourished in small groups. God can use a small group of committed Christians fully devoted to Him far more than a larger but lukewarm congregation of believers.

A small group based on the Bible can do a few key things that will differentiate it from an "encounter group" or some other psychology-based entity:

❖ share and apply the truth from God's Word;

❖ pray and intercede for one another; and

❖ use experiences from the group to develop maturity in Christ.

All small groups can grow when they include these three key activities. They can become places that bring intimacy, closeness, honesty, trust, and accountability between brothers and sisters.

There will always be those who, for one reason or another, don't want anything to do with a small group. For them, the idea of being open and transparent with a group is not something they'd want to touch with a ten-foot pole. You may feel that way as well, and if so, being involved with a small group may be uncomfortable for you at first. But it's well worth your initial discomfort. Give yourself some time to watch the dynamics within your group; as your level of trust grows, you'll find it easier to open up. Once you do, it will become still easier with practice.

ENSURING SMALL GROUP SUCCESS

There are a few things to keep in mind that will go a long way toward ensuring small group success.

Small groups need to be led by a leader (or leaders) who is capable of keeping others focused. Small groups should not be a place for gossip or murmuring. Again, much of the responsibility for directing interactions away from these things falls on small group leaders.

Confidentiality is also important—what is said in the group should stay in the group. The exception to this would be if all group participants chose to agree things could be shared outside of the group.

Finally, small groups should never pretend to be something they're not: They aren't a substitute for professional counseling, nor are they forums for expert advice on every subject, nor are they replacements for genuine marital communication (or the avoidance of all one-on-one conversation). . .nor are they able to leap tall buildings in a single bound. . .nor. . .well, you get the idea. Keep your expectations realistic.

There are a number of different types of small groups (although there may be some overlap between them). Appendix C lists the different types of small groups that exist and tells how each can help us develop as daily disciples.

SMALL GROUP PROGRESSION

O ver the course of a two- or three-year period, the progression of a small group of Christians meeting together once a week, for an hour to an hour and a half, could look like this:

❖ Commitment to the group's purpose and direction

❖ The development of close, personal relationships

❖ Freedom to share problems with confidentiality

❖ A genuine trust and concern for other members of the group

❖ An acknowledgment (and evidence) of personal spiritual growth

❖ The joy of receiving specific instruction and training through the Word

❖ Agreement by group members to hold one another accountable

❖ The ability to evaluate and act upon needed changes, through follow-up and loving concern by other brothers or sisters

❖ A hunger to follow Christ's example of servant leadership

❖ An embracing of the challenge to pass on the disciple's life

The primary reason small groups are so key to growth in Christ—to becoming a true *disciple* of Jesus—is that they are made up of committed relationships. As we discussed in an earlier chapter, God never intended us in the body of Christ to be cut off from other believers. What He desires is that we love one another, that we accept one another, that we encourage one another, and that we exhort one another.

A friend is always loyal. . .is born to help in time of need.
PROVERBS 17:17 NLT

Commitment to a regular small group of men or women is one way to live out the reality of "being one" as Jesus prayed for all believers in John 17.

Wouldn't we all want the kind of relationship that David and Jonathan had?

Because he loved him as himself.   1 SAMUEL 18:3

Through committed, small groups we have the opportunity to form this sort of relationship. We can begin down the road that leads to commitment and intimacy between the members of Christ's body—and we will mature in Christ through the process.

IT'S NEVER EASY

*But the word of the Lord continued to grow
and to be multiplied.*
ACTS 12:24 NASB

This verse appears in Acts shortly after the account of Peter's imprisonment under King Herod. Peter breaks out of jail with the assistance of an angel, then goes about his business making disciples. The verse that precedes this, verse 23, actually ends with King Herod being struck down by an angel of the Lord, and then the Scripture tells us, "and he was eaten by worms and died."

Lovely, isn't it? That's exactly how the text reads, though.

What do we make of it? Herod dies unpleasantly and then Luke, the author of Acts, tells us, "But the word of the Lord continued to grow and to be multiplied." The young church lived in times that were not always pleasant, to put it mildly, but that didn't stop them. Their leader was crucified—and things didn't get any easier from there.

Throughout the Book of Acts we read of difficult circumstances that had to be faced—conflicts, riots, and persecution.

The early Christians had to be scattered for their own safety. Still, despite these measures, Peter and John were put in jail. Stephen was stoned to death. James, the brother of John, was put to death by the sword. Peter was put in prison again. Paul was imprisoned repeatedly and on many occasions narrowly avoided being killed by the Jews.

These early disciples faced the religious and philosophical leaders of the day–people antagonistic toward the Truth but still in need of it. Worse still, the early disciples lived in a political climate where the "ruling party" didn't enjoy the emergence of new religions and was quick to act forcefully in response to uprising or conflicts. The early Christians were forced to deal with government leaders who were corrupt and ungodly–some of whom, as we see from what happened to Herod, "bit the dust" as the gospel was spread.

What can we learn?

If someone wrote a "book of Acts" about the modern Church, would the author be able to say we were faithful?

Imagine this historical account: *The president of their country was impeached.* Then the next line says, *And the believers stayed the course they were called to, didn't get distracted, didn't lose heart, but continued to grow and the number of disciples multiplied.*

The account goes on to explain our history in matter-of-fact detail. A reader someday down the road learns the importance of the story. The story includes all the facts–everything that happens, both good and bad. Through it all runs a theme that is impossible to miss. A legacy. A heritage to which we have been faithful.

In the midst of everything, the number of disciples increased through multiplication and small groups. Through commitment, investment, and godly influence, we stayed on track.

The reader of this new book of Acts learns that the modern Church, faced with amazing challenges, took a page from the early Christians who followed after Christ's death and resurrection. The modern Church in this book recognized that most of the first disciples were ordinary, working-class people. They weren't people who had any special powers of their own to spread the gospel and multiply disciples. The power the early Christians had was the same power the modern Church possesses to move mountains.

It wasn't easy. Times were tough.

But the word of the Lord continued to grow and be multiplied.

Imagine.

APPLICATIONS TO DAILY LIFE

1. What small groups have you participated in throughout your life? How would you describe these groups? Did you share and apply God's Word? Did you pray and intercede for one another? Did these groups help you develop maturity in Christ?

2. Are you involved in a small group now? Why or why not? If you are involved in a small group, how are you benefiting? Are you having a positive influence on others in the group? In what ways does the life of the group relate to your own personal life as a daily disciple?

CHAPTER 11

Leadership

Remember your leaders,
who spoke the word of God to you.
Consider the outcome of their way of life
and imitate their faith.
HEBREWS 13:7

As we have already said throughout this book, along our path as daily disciples, we are called to have godly influence on others' lives. Leadership is a part of this, for influence and leadership are intertwined.

Leadership isn't a goal every disciple will tackle automatically. If you do believe God is challenging you in the area of leadership, however, then this subject deserves your attention. If you are convinced you are not yet ready to be a leader, then read this chapter with the understanding that at some point in the future you may need to put these principles into practice.

The best leader the world has ever seen is Jesus Christ. While Christ led and affected many, the epicenter of His work as a leader was the twelve: Peter, Andrew, James (son of Zebedee), John, Philip, Bartholomew, Thomas, Matthew, James (son of Alphaeus), Thaddaeus, Simon, and Judas. Obviously, Judas decided not to respond to Christ's leadership, but the other men in this group went on to become leaders themselves in the young Church.

If no one in the body of Christ is willing to lead, the

undiscipled remain undiscipled. A leader, however, knows how to take people through a process he or she has already been through. A spiritual leader must be a mature Christian, someone who knows how to guide people through the Word. Most of all, this person must be close to Jesus so that he or she will be able to point others to Him.

SUCCESSFUL LEADERS

When I received my doctorate in 1977, my dissertation was focused on leadership. I studied coaches in football, wrestling, basketball, and track and field–and the styles they used to lead young athletes. In society we tend to perceive someone as a "winner" or "loser" simply on their win-loss record, and I studied both categories. The distinctive characteristic I observed for "winning" leaders was that they developed a style of leadership compatible with their assistant coaches, the athletic team members, and the type of sport. In other words, leaders must be adaptable and flexible in their approach. I found furthermore that leaders have a sense of vision (as we discussed in chapter five); they can "see" the finished goal. With that goal as their focus, they know how to get going and lead others through a process that ultimately brings victory. Along the way, sometimes a leadership style change is necessary, but successful leaders are able to *adapt* their approach as circumstances demand.

My research indicated that the difference between successful leaders and those who merely possess a few leadership qualities comes down to one key thing: attending to the details.

Those that could do this well were the most successful. As Chuck Swindoll has stated, "The difference between something good and something great is attention to detail."[1]

DOING OUR PART

A woman named Celia describes her experience with Christian leadership:

Tammy and I had been friends ever since our children were small when we would talk almost daily about the ongoing ups and downs of our lives. We were both Christians, and we did pray for each other. But instead of encouraging each other to grow in the Lord, we made excuses for each other. "Oh, you're doing the best you can considering how busy you are," Tammy would tell me when I would admit I felt guilty I wasn't spending more time alone with God. And I'd tell her, "Don't worry that you're not having family devotions with your kids. I don't know anyone else who really does that either."

But then Tammy moved to another state and she began to change. Now we no longer had daily phone calls, but we still talked once a week. I was glad to hear she had found a new church she loved. But then I started getting a little uneasy when she began to tell me all that she was learning from the leader of her small group. What had happened to my comfortable friend? Now, she was growing deeper with God—and she was challenging me to do the same.

I went through a time when I resented her. But then I

*opened my heart to her spiritual leadership. I'm grateful that
as she was led into a closer walk with Jesus, she took the time
to turn around and lead me right along behind her.*

Like Celia and her friend in the earlier days of their friendship, too often instead of having the courage to be spiritual
leaders, we merely give each other permission to be mediocre.
In his book *Sold Out,* Bill McCartney relates his experiences
when he came to coach the Colorado University football program in 1982, which at the time was in shambles. Despite this,
the players seemed quite content, as long as they could look
around and find someone in worse shape than they were.
McCartney states:

*We need people in our lives to challenge us, to inspire us to
greater depths of passion and greater heights of commitment.
In the same way that CU players justified their mediocrity by
comparing themselves with their teammates, I see far too
many Christians today who think and say they're OK with
Jesus. They're comfortable spiritually. And why shouldn't they
be? Looking around at all the other Christians, they see folks
much like themselves. They see them and conclude that "Hey,
I spend as much time in prayer as that guy," or "I read the
Word more than most," or "I attend church faithfully." And
they delude themselves. They have measured their walk
against someone else's standard of mediocrity. It's rampant in
the church today. Much like athletes in a middle-of-the-road
program, the church of Jesus Christ today is filled with self-
satisfied, lukewarm Christians—folks who are enamored with
the trappings of culture and the comforts of conformity.*[2]

Each of us has a responsibility. The sad reality seems to be that the mature individual–the good candidate to lead others– is scarce. And no wonder. We're too busy comforting ourselves by looking around at all the other people who aren't living up to par either.

LEADING BY SERVING

S cripture has much to say about leadership; in particular, the teachings of King Solomon in the Books of Ecclesiastes and Proverbs and King David in the Book of Psalms address this topic directly. The Bible's idea of good leadership isn't quite the same as the world's idea. In fact, the biblical concept goes against the grain of what makes sense to the world: A leader is a humble servant. Like Jesus.

Consider Christ's example, articulated beautifully in Philippians 2:3–11:

> *Do nothing out of selfish ambition or vain conceit, but in humility consider others better than yourselves. Each of you should look not only to your own interests, but also to the interests of others.*
>
> *Your attitude should be the same as that of Christ Jesus: Who, being in very nature God, did not consider equality with God something to be grasped, but made himself nothing, taking the very nature of a servant, being made in human likeness. And being found in appearance as a man, he humbled himself and became obedient to death–even death on a cross! Therefore God exalted him to the highest place and gave*

him the name that is above every name, that at the name of Jesus every knee should bow, in heaven and on earth and under the earth, and every tongue confess that Jesus Christ is Lord, to the glory of God the Father.

When is the last time you have attended a leadership seminar where the motivational speaker's topic was "Making Yourself Nothing"? What we see in the Bible, clearly, is not the world's model of leadership.

How does this affect us practically? How can we lead others in discipleship as Jesus did—by making ourselves nothing?

In the world, people are leaders simply because they have been given a job description, power, or control. This is something I'll call "positional authority leadership." The positional authoritarian often offends people, causes anxiety, and worse. Arrogance comes naturally to the person in this position, and arrogance reflects selfishness—our sin nature as human beings. The opposite of this is "functional authority leadership"—the model Christ showed when He humbled Himself as a servant leader. This sort of leader has an attitude not of selfishness but of selflessness. This leader is a good listener. . .willing to get down and dirty and do menial tasks. . .a foot-washer. The example of this leader's life is incredibly powerful. That's why this is the *best* type of leadership.

Remember that Jesus was people-oriented, not task-oriented. Others were never a means to an end for Christ; they *were* the end. In our lives as daily disciples, the purpose of having godly influence in others' lives isn't so we can get our own way. Rather, our goal is to demonstrate Christ—and bless others' lives along the way—as we develop servant-focused leadership.

KEEPING LEADERSHIP
IN PERSPECTIVE

A s we seek to *lead* (not push) another toward the disciple's life, we will have plenty of opportunities to demonstrate humility and love. Sometimes people don't *want* to be led the way of Christ; remember that God respects each person's right to decide for himself. When we are leading and discipling another, we should be careful to do so with understanding and true concern for the person rather than with a sense of superiority that attempts to hammer out change in the other's behavior.

In the Corinthian church, at the time of Paul's first letter to them, believers were confused about their real identities. Some would argue, "I'm a disciple of Paul." Others, "I am a disciple of Apollos." Still others, "Peter is the one I follow." A few of them, though, did get it right: *"I follow Christ."*

Leadership certainly is vital to the body of Christ, but no Christian's ultimate identity is ever in another person–not even a mentor. No matter who is leading and who is following within the Church, we are all disciples of Jesus. The younger or less experienced people I may lead are not *my* disciples. Nor am I a disciple of those who may mentor me along the way. Instead, we are each following Christ, encouraging one another on the journey.

PAUL'S LEADERSHIP PROGRESSION

I n the book of 2 Timothy, we see Paul giving some strong (perhaps urgent) instruction to a younger Christian. We read,

"And the things you have heard me say in the presence of many witnesses entrust to reliable men who will also be qualified to teach others" (2:2).

Notice the progression here—there are three distinct steps Paul makes:

1. "And the things you have heard," seen, experienced, witnessed, observed, and so on from mature Christian men and women (role models or leaders). . .

2. "Entrust to reliable men" or pass on to other brothers and sisters who are trustworthy and reliable to teach the gospel to the next generation of believers. . .

3. We must be "qualified to teach others." (See James 3:1 as well.) We who teach will be held to a strict standard (in other words, we have to prove we are qualified) because of the importance of our destination as disciples. As leaders, we set an example, whether we care to admit it or not, and others will follow in our steps. We don't want to lead anyone down the wrong path.

Paul is trying to convey to his understudy, Timothy, the gravity and awesome responsibility (as well as the privilege and joy) a leader has for those who receive his teaching, knowledge, and understanding. Generations of Christians to come will be the product of a faithful discipler of men and women. In modern terminology it might go something like this: "Let's do it right, and let's get it right the first time."

LEADERSHIP EXAMPLES

As stated at the beginning of the chapter, the best leader the world has ever seen is Jesus Christ. There are many other examples of great biblical leaders as well as more modern examples. In my generation I think of Winston Churchill, and a little further back in history, Abraham Lincoln. I think of Mother Teresa and St. Francis of Assisi as well as many, many other godly leaders–humble saints–many of whom were martyred. They have been used by God throughout history to "forcefully" advance His kingdom (Matthew 11:12).

ESTHER

An example of a great leader in the Bible is Queen Esther. Even when Esther knew she would face possible death if she spoke to King Xerxes unless she had been summoned into his presence, Esther's response was one of courage and devotion to God, to her cousin Mordecai, and to her Jewish people. She chose to approach her husband, the king, anyway, for this action was necessary to save the lives of the Jews.

> *Then Esther sent this reply to Mordecai: "Go, gather together all the Jews who are in Susa, and fast for me. Do not eat or drink for three days, night or day. I and my maids will fast as you do. When this is done, I will go to the king, even though it is against the law. And if I perish, I perish."*
>
> ESTHER 4:15–16

Because of Esther's leadership and commitment, the Jews were delivered from death. She exposed the evil plan of Haman, one of the king's nobles, to extinguish the Jewish race. The Jews' sorrow was turned into joy–their mourning into a day of celebration.

Esther was obviously concerned for her own well-being. Who wouldn't be? But her concern for *others first* made the difference in her life.

When you are faced with a huge obstacle, how do you react? Do you put yourself first. . .or others? Are you a true leader like Esther?

DEBORAH

Before the days of Esther, Deborah was another rare female leader–"a mother in Israel" according to Judges 5:7. God, through Deborah's leadership, helped Israel win a battle against their Canaanite antagonists. Deborah was the one who led the plan to overtake Sisera, the leader of the Canaanite army.

The unique thing about Deborah was that she didn't view herself as a leader per se, but as a motherly, parental figure over Israel's people. In the absence of any official crown or title, Deborah cared enough about her people to allow God to use her to lead.

Even for those of us who do not view ourselves as having an influential position of leadership, we can still be a mother or father type of leader to those around us. Deborah's example shows we can lead others in the right direction, even when normal circumstances wouldn't suggest we'd be the most likely leaders.

DAVID

If I could point to one biblical example of a leader as my favorite, it would have to be David. I can relate to David and the story of his mighty men: Josheb, Eleazar, and Shammah (the "top three"), and the thirty others he had under him who would fight for him to the death because of all he had done for them.

Ultimately, David was a good leader because he was a man after God's own heart (1 Samuel 13:14, Acts 13:22). With David, life wasn't about style over substance. The Bible explains why David was a leader: "The LORD does not look at the things man looks at. Man looks at the outward appearance, but the LORD looks at the heart" (1 Samuel 16:7). I believe David was a good leader *first* because he was *honest* with God. *Second*, he was *courageous* as evidenced with Goliath. *Third*, he was *repentant* when he sinned against God with Bathsheba. And *fourth*, he was a *lover* of God; Psalm 51 reveals David had a humble spirit (though he was a leader) and a longing to be with God.

> *The sacrifices of God are a broken spirit; a broken and contrite heart, O God, you will not despise.* PSALM 51:17

David didn't just know *about* God. He *knew* God and loved him with all his heart, soul, and strength.

And people followed.

Are you a man or woman after God's heart?

MAKING A DIFFERENCE

We can all be a leader to somebody, whether our spouses, children, siblings, friends, coworkers—chances are, someone is looking up to us. Biblically, we have the responsibility and calling to be good leaders. We can either accept it or ignore it.

Musician Ray Boltz wrote a song a few years ago called "Thank You." In this song, he tells about a Sunday school teacher who taught him of Jesus; through this teacher, Boltz became a Christian. This song conveys an important truth: There are multitudes of unsung heroes–people whom the world never noticed as leaders, but who made all of the difference for Christ in other people's lives. They are truly "the greatest leaders," because they were humble and focused on Jesus; they cared about others and acted out their love in concrete ways. As we are told in the Book of James, "As the body without the spirit is dead, so faith without deeds is dead" (2:26). This isn't legalism. This is reality. We can't lead without others being able to see the love tangibly evident in our lives.

In his classic book, *The Master Plan of Evangelism,* Robert Coleman says this:

> *The world is desperately seeking someone to follow. That they will follow someone is certain, but will that person be one who knows the way to Christ, or will he or she be one like themselves, leading them only on to greater darkness? This is the decisive question of our plan of life. The relevance of all that we do waits on its verdict, and in turn, the destiny of the multitudes hangs in the balance.*[3]

Where are you at today? Are you ready to take your place as a leader? Or are you waiting for something?

The body of Christ needs good leadership. . .now.

How will you live from here on?

Daily DISCIPLES

APPLICATIONS TO DAILY LIFE

1. Who are the people in your life who have been spiritual leaders for you? Did they lead with "positional authority"? Or were they servant leaders like Jesus? If they were servant leaders, in what ways did they serve?

2. With which biblical leader (Esther, Deborah, or David) do you identify most? Why?

3. Who in your life might benefit from your leadership?

CHAPTER 12

Not a 100-Meter Dash but a Marathon

Mass crusades,
in which I believe and to which I have committed my life,
will never finish the Great Commission;
but a one-by-one ministry will.[1]
BILLY GRAHAM

I n October of 1996 I was privileged to be a part of a team of
Promise Keepers' staff who were charged with traveling
across each one of the Hawaiian Islands over a thirteen-day
period. We were to contact churches, pastors, and men about
attending the Promise Keepers conference to be held in January
of the following year in Honolulu.

While we were on this whirlwind tour of the islands, something unique happened to me while I was on the "Big Island."
As we were traveling from Hilo to Kona, we literally found ourselves right in the middle of the Iron Man Triathlon, which is
held annually in Kona.

The Iron Man, of course, is one of the most physically grueling events in the entire world. Drawing fifteen hundred participants, both male and female, from around the world, it pits
competitors in three back-to-back tests of endurance: a 2½-mile
ocean swim, a 112-mile bicycle race along the road–and through
sweltering lava beds–and then a 26.2-mile marathon run to top it
all off. The upper tier of finishers complete this astounding
triathlon in nine to twelve hours, while some finish in eighteen to

twenty-two hours—nearly a full day of constant physical activity. It's a sight simply to behold, especially when you consider the amount of training that each participant had to go through before he or she could even attempt such grueling exercise.

The disciple's life is a little like that. Daily disciples experience ongoing training and action, training and action. They constantly rethink and rearrange their priorities; they are prepared and persevering. But we don't become discipled Christians through any single encounter—anymore than those athletes could prepare for the Iron Man in one training session.

A woman named Terri, who is both a businessperson and a homemaker, discusses these same ideas in a slightly different context:

I'm not always good at waiting for the long-term goals in my life. I want instant results now. But in my career I had to learn that overnight I wouldn't arrive at my ultimate goal; I had to be patient and work hard where I was at now, rather than keeping my eyes always focused on some point years in the future. If I didn't want to spend my time being frustrated and discouraged, I had to enjoy the work here and now, knowing that it would eventually lead me forward to my long-range goals.

When I became a mother, the same principle applied. Raising children is a process, a lifelong process—and you have to enjoy the journey. (It wouldn't make much sense to say, "I won't be satisfied until my children are all grown up. Only then will I allow myself to enjoy them.") No, as a parent, you have to work hard and be vigilant each step along the way—and each step is full of its own unique joys.

And now at last, I'm learning that this same principle

*applies to my walk with God. My spiritual life used to go in
fits and starts. I'd get excited and inspired—but then I'd
become discouraged and frustrated with myself, because I still
seemed so far from being all God wanted me to be. Finally,
though, I'm beginning to understand that just like in my
business, just like with my children, following God is a
process, a lifelong one. I have to work hard along the way,
and I have to keep my focus on the long-term goal—but I also
have to understand that God walks with me here and now,
as I grow step by step.*

In recent years we've seen an immense increase in the number of men and women who have attended events and come away energized and challenged in their faith. But this cannot be the end. As Terri learned, we are called to a daily life of disciplehood, not just an awakening.

The disciple's life starts one person at a time, one family at a time, one church at a time, one community at a time. . .and then one nation at a time. The legacy Christ left with His disciples is an ongoing one—to the glory of God.

What a legacy He has left us! By any measuring standard, Jesus' legacy stands alone. As Philip Yancey observed, "You can gauge the size of a ship that has passed out of sight by the huge wake it leaves behind."[2] Christ began with twelve men. Today millions know His name.

We can sit back and marvel at this. But we also need to realize that this process took time and a great deal of *intentional* effort.

Will we make the same commitment today? Do we have a plan?

Even as I came to work today I had to take a specific path

across various avenues, streets, and freeways to get to my workplace. I don't wander back and forth on my way to work. I have a sense of direction. I know I need to follow a certain path if I'm going to end up where I should. In the same way, there are no shortcuts or quick fixes to the process of disciplehood. Instead, it's a daily lifestyle.

In the body of Christ, sometimes in our zeal to evangelize, the message of personal ongoing discipleship gets lost. In our hurry-up world we like things to be "instant," but this sort of thinking just doesn't apply to the Kingdom of God. Theologian A. W. Tozer sums it up well:

> *Instant Christianity tends to make the faith act terminal and so smothers the desire for spiritual advance. It fails to understand the true nature of the Christian life, which is not static but dynamic and expanding. It overlooks the fact that a new Christian is a living organism as certainly as a new baby is, and must have nourishment and exercise to assure normal growth. It does not consider that the act of faith in Christ sets up a personal relationship between two intelligent moral beings, God and the reconciled man, and no single encounter between God and a creature made in His image could ever be sufficient to establish an intimate friendship between them. . . .*
>
> *Undue preoccupation with the initial act of believing has created in some a psychology of contentment, or at least of non-expectation. To many it has imparted a mood of disappointment with the Christian faith. God seems too far away, the world is too near, and the flesh too powerful to resist. Others are glad to accept the assurance of automatic blessedness. It relieves them of the need to watch and fight and pray, and sees them free to enjoy this world while awaiting the next.*[3]

Daily DISCIPLES

Perhaps the best way to stay active in the disciple's daily marathon is to have an end goal always in mind. A good way to focus here is to think about what you would like to see written as your epitaph. If we knew our lives would end today, what would we want (or what could we expect) our family or friends to engrave on our headstones?

We must take a good look at ourselves and ask, *Have I lived up to, and accomplished, what God commissioned me to do?*

An epitaph is like a summary statement at the end of our lives. How could we condense our entire life into a single statement on a gravestone? It's like the personal vision statement we discussed in chapter 5–only written from hindsight.

I have thought about this, and I would want my gravestone to say: "He loved God and was a discipler of others." If that statement is characteristic of my life and a true representation of my spiritual walk and who I was, then I believe I could assess my life as effective, especially in God's eyes (although maybe not the world's). My vision for my life is to make this epitaph a true one.

You may want your epitaph to read differently. It may be a variation of mine. But you must seek to set the course of your life accordingly. Whatever we do, whatever shape our "visions" for our lives take, we are all called to run the disciple's daily marathon "in such a way as to get the prize. . .to get a crown that will last forever" (1 Corinthians 9:24–25).

It's not about words on a piece of stone.

It's about what kind of life you are living.

Do you choose to be a daily disciple?

APPLICATIONS TO DAILY LIFE

1. In what areas of your life have you learned to be patient,
    working hard along the way while you work toward a
    long-term goal? Do you ever feel discouraged or frus-
    trated? Do you think God is discouraged or frustrated
    with you? What do you need to do to please Him?

If you were to honestly write your epitaph today, what would
you say? If you were to write it several years from now, would
it be any different? What do you want your legacy to be?

APPENDIX A

Spiritual Gifts Inventory

A s we have said throughout this book, being Christ's disciple is not a solitary activity. The Kingdom of God is a kingdom of love—and love is made real within the context of relationships. Some of us may prefer to rely on our own strength, not needing anyone else, but we are not called to be independent; we are meant to need each other. As members of the Church, we are parts of Christ's body—and each body part is dependent on all the others. When the body works together, each member functioning in harmony with all the others, then it is healthy and effective.

In the same way that each part of our physical body has its own unique strengths and function, each member of Christ's body also has unique qualities and abilities. We often refer to these as spiritual gifts. If we are to be strong, functioning body members, we all need to practice our own special spiritual gifts. This is an important aspect of daily discipleship.

But before you can put your spiritual gift to work, you need to be aware of what it is. Here are some general principles about spiritual gifts:

❖ Believe that you have at least one gift. (1 Peter 4:10)

❖ Realize that the Holy Spirit gave you your gift(s).
(1 Corinthians 12:7, 11)

❖ Understand the purpose of your gift(s).

❖ Desire to know and use your gift. (1 Corinthians 14:1, 12)

❖ Be controlled by the Holy Spirit. (Ephesians 5:18–21)

❖ Don't worry about the Holy Spirit's work! (Philippians 2:13)

❖ Evaluate carefully which gift(s) you desire to use and which gift's (gifts') use brings you joy and a sense of effectiveness. (Psalm 37:4)

❖ Be available at all times to serve and to use the gift(s) you believe you have.

❖ Be in consistent prayer and study of the Word, seeking the Lord's will and His glory as you exercise your gift(s). (1 Peter 4:10–11)

❖ Seek wisdom and advice from mature believers and church leaders. (Hebrews 13:7, 17)

When mature believers indicate that your ministry is not effective, have the courage to examine their judgment objectively—and then, if need be, accept it and explore other gifts.

After you have been putting your gift to use for a while and have achieved a level of maturity, seek the wisdom and advice of others as to what they have observed and how they feel about you.

❖ Accept God's chain of command (whether in your family, church, business, school, or government) as a key to revealing His will for your life. (Ephesians 5:21–22, 25, 6:1; Titus 3:1; Hebrews 13:7, 17)

❖ Don't exalt the gift–give all the glory to God.
(1 Corinthians 10:31; 1 Peter 4:11)

❖ Whatever purpose God has for you on this earth, you have the capacity to accomplish that task for Him. (Romans 8:28)

SPIRITUAL GIFTS AS DESCRIBED IN SCRIPTURE

(ROMANS 12:6–8)

❖ prophecy
❖ serving
❖ teaching
❖ encouraging

❖ giving
❖ leadership
❖ mercy

(1 CORINTHIANS 12:1–11)

❖ wisdom
❖ knowledge
❖ faith
❖ healing
❖ ability to distinguish between spirits

❖ miracles
❖ prophecy
❖ speaking in tongues
❖ interpretation of tongues

WHAT ARE YOUR PERSONAL SPIRITUAL GIFTS FROM GOD?

Here are some principles to keep in mind as you identify your spiritual gifts:

❖ God doesn't ask a man or woman to do what He hasn't *equipped* him or her to do.

❖ Don't try to be what you're not; develop the gifts *you have.*

❖ On a sheet of paper, write out what you think your gifts are.

Sometimes we can identify our spiritual gifts as we look at the way that different personal qualities function in our lives. Here are some aspects of spiritual gifts to keep in mind:

❖ Gifts should produce *maturity, growth,* and *unity* in the church.

❖ Spiritual gifts are to be used "to *prepare* God's people for *works of service,* so that the *body of Christ* may be *built up.*" (Ephesians 4:12, emphasis added)

❖ Peter states in Acts 3:6, " 'Silver or gold I do not have, but what I have I give you. In the name of Jesus Christ of Nazareth, walk.' " Proper use of spiritual gifts leads to sharing, *building up the body* of Christ by helping others; spiritual gifts are not intended for *self-improvement* or *private use.* These gifts are to be shared, not hoarded.

As you go forward with identifying and developing your gifts, be sure to consult with other mature disciples who know you well and glean from their counsel.

THE PURPOSE OF VARIOUS SPIRITUAL GIFTS

1. Apostles for the ministry of the Word

2. Prophecy to equip God's people

3. Teaching

4. Workers of miracles for the ministry of the spectacular

5. Healing to explain God's truth

6. Evangelism

7. Encouragement

8. Contributing to the needs of others

9. Leadership for the ministry of helping

10. Mercy to enable God's work

11. Administration

12. Wisdom

13. Knowledge

14. Faith

15. Discerning of spirits for the ministry of special gifts

16. Tongues to establish God's authority

17. Interpretation of tongues

APPENDIX B

Twenty-Six Commands to Heed as a Daily Disciple of Christ
(Romans 12:9–21)

1. Let love be sincere.

2. Hate evil.

3. Cling to what is good.

4. Be devoted to one another.

5. Honor others above self.

6. Never lack zeal.

7. Keep spiritual fervor.

8. Serve the Lord.

9. Be joyful in hope.

10. Be patient in affliction.

11. Be faithful in prayer.

12. Share with God's people in need.

13. Practice hospitality.

14. Bless those who persecute you.

15. Rejoice with those who rejoice.

16. Mourn with those who mourn.

17. Live in harmony with one another.

18. Do not be proud.

19. Associate with people of low position.

20. Do not be conceited.

21. Do not repay evil for evil.

22. Be careful to live in an honest, aboveboard way.

23. Live in peace with everyone. (If it is at all possible!)

24. Do not take revenge.

25. Do not be overcome by evil.

26. Overcome evil with good.

Small Group Variations

THE PRAYER GROUP

A prayer group can be composed of a larger number of people than the standard small group. (I've seen one as large as fifty participants.) In a prayer group, though, the leader must set some parameters or lay down enough guidelines to keep some semblance of order.

There are a number of options for prayer groups. Some I've seen are:

1. quiet prayer groups where individual participants pray silently;

2. groups that pray out loud;

3. intercessory groups;

4. groups that focus on prayer walks or vigils;

5. conversational or topical theme prayer groups; and

6. committed "prayer partner" groups.

All of us should be involved in prayer—clearly it's a core part of living as a daily disciple—but I believe God has given some people the charge to be real prayer warriors. These are the kinds of people who are most likely to be in prayer groups. This sort of group can help us as a guide through our spiritual journey, at whatever point we are in the disciple's life.

BIBLE STUDY GROUP

A Bible study group meets to do just that—study God's Word in a specific fashion. Through group consensus, the members select a book or theme in the Bible to study. Ideally a leader will be designated to oversee the direction and function of the study. The leader should provide various supplementary input (from study guides, concordances, commentaries, and other sources) to give insight into the content and background of the book or portion of the Bible being studied.

Another direction a Bible study group can go is what I call a special topic group. This group looks to the Word as well as to current information or study guides on their topic of interest. For example, if a group wanted to study about the "heart," they could begin by looking at an exhaustive concordance listing of the number of times "heart" is listed in the Bible, and begin to review the context and content of the references. Then, various study guides as well as group discussion can add perspective. In addition, many dissertations and themes have been written on the topic of the heart.

All of these can add to the learning process of the topic of study (whether it be the heart or something else). We are truly blessed in today's world to have such a vast amount of knowledge at our fingertips. Many Bible software discs contain exhaustive amounts of information for our personal computers.

Then, of course, we can also take advantage of the ever-growing world of the Internet. Mature Christians need an understanding of countless issues. In the special topic group context, fellowship with other believers can help bring understanding and knowledge to these issues.

Studying the Bible in a group context can be a time of fellowship and developing relationships—for any Christian at any point in the disciple's life.

Encouragement/Accountability Group

An encouragement/accountability group emerges when men or women become transparent and begin to open up to those in the group, through mutual trust.

Christians struggle with sin. Consequently, we normally try to resist any kind of true accountability that might expose our faults. Still, sometimes we get to the point in our spiritual and relational lives where we desire to be totally honest and open with another individual. This is something more than a surface relationship; this is where we come to the point that we realize the face we put on every day is beginning to look worn—where we realize a need to explore some of the deeper life issues with which we struggle.

The decision to invite another person to "hold our feet to the fire" is, initially, a difficult thing to do; it's even harder to trust a group of people that much. Allowing a group access to those areas of our life where we are vulnerable, giving them permission to encourage us to make a change in our behavior when needed. . .well, all that can be very, *very* difficult.

When there is love within the encouragement/accountability group, participants give one another the best advice on how they can each change for the better and become more mature and Christlike. After being in a group like this and experiencing the challenge and change, I can say that I will never be without the counsel of the members of an encouragement/accountability group again. This sort of group can help the process of being a daily disciple. Working through our struggles together and being honest and open to counsel, we become more mature in Christ.

DISCIPLESHIP GROUP

P erhaps this is an "odd" category, considering that this entire book is dedicated to discipleship. While the end result of small group relationships of any kind should be growth through Christian fellowship, a discipleship group has a specific, intentional focus on two key areas.

The first is mentoring and leadership. By example, the leader of this group is an individual who demonstrates maturity through servanthood—and he or she will attempt to model that for others in the group. Usually this is an older person.

The second key area is an emphasis on the spiritual growth process, with the overriding goal being directed by verses such as 1 Peter 2:2 ("Like newborn babies, crave pure spiritual milk, so that by it you may grow up in your salvation. . ."); 1 Corinthians

3:1–2 ("Brothers, I could not address you as spiritual but as worldly—mere infants in Christ. I gave you milk, not solid food, for you were not yet ready for it. Indeed, you are still not ready"); and Hebrews 5:12–14 ("In fact, though by this time you ought to be teachers, you need someone to teach you the elementary truths of God's word all over again. You need milk, not solid food! Anyone who lives on milk, being still an infant, is not acquainted with the teaching about righteousness. But solid food is for the mature, who by constant use have trained themselves to distinguish good from evil").

Scripture contrasts infants to mature believers who, through regular use and study of the Word, have trained themselves to be Christlike disciples. A discipleship group focuses specifically on the process described in 2 Timothy 2:15: "Do your best to present yourself to God as one approved, a workman who does not need to be ashamed and who correctly handles the word of truth."

SPECIAL INTEREST GROUP

S pecial interest groups (not to be confused with the political lobbying kind) focus on reaching out to individuals who have interest in a specific area.

For example: How do you reach out with the gospel to someone who loves riding motorcycles? How do you reach out to the mother who has three small children at home? What about the man or woman who golfs? Then there's the person who likes to hunt and fish but never goes to church—what about this individual?

Many special organizations have been raised up as para-church ministries to come alongside the Church in presenting and implementing the gospel of Jesus Christ. M.O.P.s (Mothers of Preschoolers) is an example of this; it's an organization designed to give support to young mothers, while also spreading the gospel. Groups like this provide specific information that is spiritually relevant for non-Christians as well as Christians. Countless men and women receive Jesus as Savior and Lord through special interest groups that focus on those areas to which people are naturally drawn; many of these are individuals who would not normally be caught dead in a church pew on Sunday. Through special interest groups, the disciple's life is introduced to a much wider audience than merely those who attend local services. These groups are also places where those who share a common interest can use it as a catalyst to relate and grow together in Christ.

SERVICE GROUP

Jesus said in Matthew 20:28, " 'Just as the Son of Man did not come to be served, but to serve, and to give his life as a ransom for many.' " As we grow in our faith, in the knowledge of God, and in the tenets of our church, again we should realize that God saved us to serve, not sit. A service group *serves* in the community in various capacities, whether it be working with the homeless in a local shelter, running a crisis pregnancy clinic, stocking a food bank, or working in any number of other areas of need.

Many Christians are delighted to be on the receiving end of

things, but few are regular "foot-washers" on the serving end of relationships. Yet we are called to bless others by allowing the Lord to use us as servants to the needs of others. As the Word states in John 13:14–17, " 'Now that I, your Lord and Teacher, have washed your feet, you also should wash one another's feet. I have set you an example that you should do as I have done for you. I tell you the truth, no servant is greater than his master, nor is a messenger greater than the one who sent him. Now that you know these things, you will be blessed if you do them.' " True joy and blessing come as we, without ulterior motives, choose to meet the needs others may have. Through a service group, we can demonstrate the committed servanthood Christ exhibited. After all, His life is the example we are called to emulate in our lives as daily disciples.

SMALL GROUPS 101

A group can move out into different directions, too. What started out as a prayer group might evolve into a service group—or vice versa. And again, there may be some overlap between the different types of groups. A Bible study group might decide to participate in an intentional service activity, or perhaps the service group may develop into an encouragement/account-ability group. A group can start off open to any new members and then become closed. Or maybe the group is closed to new members to begin, but then evolves to the point where group members desire to open up to new participants.

Small groups ideally should consist of around four to ten people. If the participants in the group get along well, that's certainly helpful; however, the group shouldn't be limited to just close friends. God can and does develop new friendships–lasting ones–through small group fellowship.

When it comes to a meeting place for small groups, a group needs to be able to have privacy. In particular, this is very important if there will be any sensitive subject matter shared during group meetings.

Another important facet of small groups is making sure that a clear purpose is established. For instance, if half of the participants are looking for a challenge in their spiritual lives, but the other half would just prefer to be entertained, there is a problem. Further, groups should make note of the progress made toward growth in Christ and the development of relationships. If no progress can be detected, it may be time to reevaluate. A small group shouldn't be strictly a place for socializing. Friendship and camaraderie are good things; but–dare I say it?–the purpose of small groups should be more "biblical" than some of the things that tend to occupy our chatter as human beings.

Lastly, I believe it is crucial that groups meet regularly. I know of one man who shared with me a story about the lack of success his church group experienced when it attempted to get a men's ministry going. They decided to meet once a month. Meeting so seldom is a recipe for a quick fizzle. Obviously, we face some obstacles when we seek a time to which everyone can commit. If attendance is poor or deteriorates, experimentation with different times or meeting places may be necessary. But–and this is key–*don't give up!*

NOTES

CHAPTER 1

1. Oswald Chambers, *My Utmost for His Highest*, Discovery House Publishers (Grand Rapids, MI), 1963, p. 115.

2. Steve Farrar, *Finishing Strong*, Multnomah Books (Sisters, OR), 1996, p. 5.

CHAPTER 2

1. Jack Hayford, "Uniting Together as Brothers in Christ" presentation, Promise Keepers Men's Conference (Seattle, WA), 1996.

CHAPTER 3

1. C.S. Lewis, quoted in *Men of Integrity* devotional, Christianity Today, Inc. (Carol Stream, IL), March/April 1999, March 3.

2. Dr. Gary Rosberg, *Guard Your Heart*, Multnomah Books (Sisters, OR), 1994, p. 128.

3. Geoff Gorsuch and Dan Schaffer, *Brothers! Calling Men into Vital Relationships*, NavPress (Colorado Springs, CO), 1994, pp. 51–52.

4. Larry Burkett and Rick Osborne, quoted in *New Man* magazine, Strang Communications (Lake Mary, FL), May 1997, p. 23.

5. Dr. Richard Halverson, quoted in the book *Bonds of Iron*, James

Osterhaus, Ph.D., Moody Press (Chicago, IL), 1994, p. 92.

CHAPTER 5

1. Chambers, *My Utmost for His Highest*, p. 188.

2. Helen Keller, quoted in the book *Tender Warrior*, Stu Weber, Multnomah Books (Sisters, OR), 1993, p. 21.

3. Chambers, *My Utmost for His Highest*, p. 188.

CHAPTER 6

1. *USA Weekend* survey, quoted in the book *True Stories of Answered Prayer: God's Response to Famous and Everyday People*, Mike Nappa, Tyndale House Publishers (Grand Rapids, MI), 1999, introduction page.

CHAPTER 8

1. Gene Getz, *Building Up One Another*, Victor Books (Colorado Springs, CO), 1997, pp. 21–22.

2. *The Denver Post*, "Black and white together," 2/12/98, p. 10B.

CHAPTER 9

1. Gary Smalley and John Trent, *The Blessing*, Pocket Books (New York, NY), 1991, pp. 27–33.

2. Farrar, *Finishing Strong*, p. 106.

CHAPTER 10

1. George Barna, "The State of the American Church: An Assessment of the Need for Spiritual Revival" presentation, Vision 2000 Summit (Denver, CO), 1998.

CHAPTER 11

1. Chuck Swindoll, quoted in the book *The Promise Keeper at Work,* Bob Horner, Ron Ralston, and Dave Sunde, Focus on the Family Publishing (Colorado Springs, CO), 1996, p. 51.

2. Bill McCartney with David Halbrook, *Sold Out: Becoming Man Enough to Make a Difference,* Word Publishing (Nashville, TN), 1997, p. 143.

3. Robert E. Coleman, *The Master Plan of Evangelism,* Fleming H. Revell (Grand Rapids, MI), 1994, p. 116.

CHAPTER 12

1. Billy Graham, *The Holy Spirit,* Word Books (Dallas, TX), 1978, p. 147.

2. Philip Yancey, *The Jesus I Never Knew,* Zondervan Publishing House (Grand Rapids, MI), 1995, p. 17.

3. A. W. Tozer, *The Best of A. W. Tozer,* Christian Publications (Camp Hill, PA), 1995, p. 105.

Afterword

I'm not saying that I have this all together, that I have it made. But I am well on my way, reaching out for Christ, who has so wondrously reached out for me. Friends, don't get me wrong: By no means do I count myself an expert in all of this, but I've got my eye on the goal, where God is beckoning us onward—to Jesus. I'm off and running, and I'm not turning back.

So let's keep focused on that goal, those of us who want everything God has for us. If any of you have something else in mind, something less than total commitment, God will clear your blurred vision—you'll see it yet! Now that we're on the right track, let's stay on it.

Stick with me, friends. Keep track of those you see running this same course, headed for this same goal. There are many out there taking other paths, choosing other goals, and trying to get you to go along with them. I've warned you of them many times; sadly, I'm having to do it again. All they want is easy street. They hate Christ's Cross. But easy street is a dead-end street. Those who live there make their bellies their gods; belches are their praise; all they can think of is their appetites.

But there's far more to life for us. We're citizens of high heaven! We're waiting the arrival of the Savior, the Master,

221

Jesus Christ, who will transform our earthly bodies into glorious bodies like his own. He'll make us beautiful and whole with the same powerful skill by which he is putting everything as it should be, under and around him.

PHILIPPIANS 3:12–21 THE MESSAGE

PRESS ON!

ABOUT THE AUTHORS

David Wardell is the cofounder of the international ministry Promise Keepers and currently serves as ambassador-at-large. Dave earned his Ph.D. at the University of Utah. He has also served as an assistant professor at the University of Colorado and has taught at Kansas State University.

Jeff Leever has worked as a writer and editor for numerous publications. He currently serves as editor for *Men of Integrity,* a devotional magazine copublished by Promise Keepers and *Christianity Today.* Formerly senior editor for Promise Keepers, Jeff now acts as manager of publications.

ALSO AVAILABLE FROM
DR. DAVID WARDELL AND JEFFREY A. LEEVER

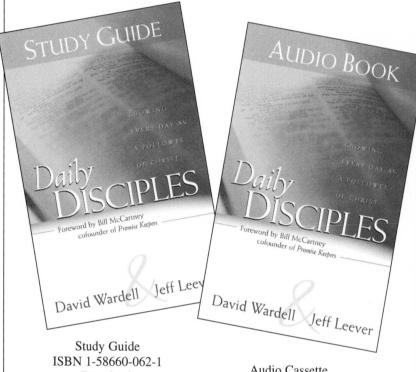

Study Guide
ISBN 1-58660-062-1
Paperback
$4.99

Audio Cassette
ISBN 1-58660-061-3
$14.99

AVAILABLE
WHEREVER BOOKS ARE SOLD

PROMISE
PRESS